THE NEW YORK I KNOW

The New York I Know

BY MARYA MANNES

WITH PHOTOGRAPHS BY

HERB SNITZER

J.B. LIPPINCOTT COMPANY

PHILADELPHIA AND NEW YORK

My thanks to The Reporter *magazine*
for letting me pick this assignment
and for running it as I wrote it.
M. M.

First Edition

Library of Congress Catalog Card Number 61-12195
Manufactured in the United States of America

to

Christopher

Also by Marya Mannes: MORE IN ANGER

CONTENTS

PREFACE

WHAT I feel about New York is written here. Why I have written it is another matter. In a sense it is a form of exorcism, in a sense a search for the roots of my love for, and hate of, this city. I have lived here since I was born, and although it may not be possible to sink real roots in this drilled and blasted rock as one would in untampered earth, New York is in my bones. I have lived for times in many other places, mostly in Europe, with pleasure and gain. But I have never thought of myself as anything but a New Yorker.

For the first long span, this involvement was largely love. New York was to me the most exciting and important place in the world. And though our family left it on many Junes for long summers abroad, the first returning sight of the city from the Narrows brought a rush of joy. Later, the cab ride home up Tenth Avenue shadowed this: it was impossible not to compare it sadly with the streets of Paris or Salzburg or Amsterdam. But once that hurdle was safely passed, the old pride returned.

I have tried to fix the date when it began to waiver, when I began to worry and wonder about this town, to resist it, to cast a cold and critical eye; and I believe the end of World War II marked the beginning. The beginning of what? Of that point, I think, when a city can no longer cope with its people, when—through overcrowding, inefficiency, corruption, and greed—it sacrifices, for the limitless pursuit of financial profit, those amenities which spell civilized living. It is a point of strangulation, of brutality against the individual, of ferocious tension; and if proof of this condition were wanted, a walk on unfashionable streets or a ride in the subway would provide it. This city is full of fragmented people, from those who talk to themselves and move jerkily to those whose faces are set in hostility or negation. The population of New York is not a gay one: it is too busy fighting to survive.

There are many, I know, who do not feel this. They are the very successful who can afford to cushion themselves with money against the myriad discomforts of our streets, who are chauffeur-driven to work, who pay dearly to be served in uncrowded restaurants and see plays in the best seats, who live high above the tumult, who can save their energies for the exhilaration of fighting on the highest levels of business or profession.

There are those, too—thousands of them—who have never known New York as it used to be, and who find it so far superior to the cities and towns of their birth and childhood that they accept it without reservation. And there are those who, never having lived in London or Paris or Rome, do not know what civilized living in a city can be.

For the young on their way up, New York is still the sum of their dreams. For the tourist it is still the greatest show on earth. And for the educated foreigner it is often an intoxication of freedom, a ka-

10

leidoscope of those shifting delights—of anonymity and discovery—which the traditional pattern of his life at home does not permit him.

All these loves of New York I understand. I understand even more that the unceasing ferment of this town is creative as well as destructive. If the talent of America is not born here, it usually flowers here, for this is the stimulus, the forcing ground, and the market place.

It is also many things of which I have not written here, not for lack of interest but for lack of that interior knowledge which is, I hope, the premise of this book. Wall Street, the Lower East Side, Harlem, the Bronx, Chelsea, Gramercy Park—I have seen them, but I have not lived with them, and what I could tell about them would be told in detachment.

Of the New York I know, I have celebrated its beauties and excitements as often as I have dwelt on its ugliness. It is a prodigious city, and prodigiously interesting. While I am strong and productive, there is no other city I could accept as my home without a sense of exile. For those fortunate enough, or determined enough, to make their own worlds, it is possible to take the best that New York can offer by holding up a deliberate shield against its dirt, its corruption, and its indignities. It is possible, but not easy, to avert the eye from the filth on the sidewalk, the spit on the streets, and the decay that blights whole areas of the city. It is possible, but not easy, to endure with patience the

twenty minutes needed to ride one block because of

illegal parking and loading, and to wait ten minutes on an icy corner for a bus that drives by without stopping. It is possible, but not easy, to accept criminality and discourtesy as by-products of a huge and affluent city. It is possible, and only too easy, to deny the open concentration camp that is Harlem.

It is possible, too, to believe that the nadir of these various uglinesses may have been reached. People in the city are rising against them, whether they are planners drafting new areas to supplant blight or citizens bent on the salvage of the young and lost, the sick and lonely, the alien and the old, or the decent many who cannot live in the city of their choice if they must choose between luxury, which they cannot afford, and squalor, which they will not afford. And all through the city, young people are now fighting for a new vigor and direction in city government, no longer able to tolerate the weakness and confusion and cowardice and venality of the entrenched political machine. It is possible, but not easy, to believe that New York may have begun its arduous upward path, and that ten years may see not only a city of glass but a better way of living.

If not, it may become a place to shun, a giant trap inviting its own destruction. Until either future, this New Yorker has set down one image of the city, deeply held. And if there should be, at the core of this image, one quality above all which marks New York apart from all other great cities and which cannot be described, it is the atmosphere of potential. Above the towers the ceiling is unlimited.

1. *The West Seventies*

AT FOUR O'CLOCK in the morning—not before and not after—the only sound on Central Park West in the seventies is the clopping of horses' hooves. It is the homeward run of one of the Plaza broughams, and it is the only sound—apart from the bull roar of ocean liners, outward bound—that has remained constant since my youth on the West Side.

The time of it, to be sure, is different, since children are not awake at four in the morning, listening. The hooves were heard in the daytime in the Park, and with any luck close by; for it was a major treat during childhood convalescences to ride in an open victoria in the bright still air. And the clopping was loud because no other sound, in those simple days, was louder, except for the purring of a snub-nosed Renault or a lordly Pierce-Arrow down the empty avenues.

Now this sound of hooves is a profoundly melancholy evocation. The horse, you know as you lie in the dark, is not only an anachronism but a freak. Not only a freak, but a worn-out, spavined, low-headed, spiritless beast; and you wonder how he stands that last long pull to his stable at that hour. He is really half dead.

The West Seventies And the West Side I once knew is wholly dead, the tale of what has happened to it in thirty-five years a parable of decline, harshly tangible. And if the West Side I speak of here is only one small segment of the long strip that borders the Hudson on one side and Central Park and Fifth Avenue on the other, it suffers the same sickness as the rest, and contains, perhaps, greater and closer extremes of wealth and poverty than other parts.

Only one factor of the West Sixties and Seventies has remained constant in the last decades: ugliness. Except for two views—of the great River and the variable Park—there is nothing in the streets or avenues to excite or solace the eye. Three buildings only were awesome to a child: the Dakota Apartments at Seventy-second Street and Central Park West, the Museum of Natural History five blocks north, and the Schwab Mansion on Riverside Drive. None had beauty, but the first two are still heavily impressive in the Victorian manner: massive, thick-walled, ornamented, and somber. The last, a monstrous pile in bastardized château style, has long since been razed and supplanted by a huge apartment complex. But at least it was grandiose and mysterious, and the lawns through the iron railings were brilliantly green and velvet-smooth.

The dullness of houses and apartments fronting the Hudson were—and are—redeemed by the majestic sweep of the River and the rocky wall of the Jersey side, defaced and cluttered though it is by the cheap accidents of private greed, bereft, in the manner of most of our cities, of public vision. It is one of the social ironies of Manhattan that the grand prospects and superior air of Riverside Drive should

16

have been shunned, even in my time, by the fashionable and the rich, to whom the right address with the right neighbors is worth any price in cash and congestion. "Nice" people lived on Riverside Drive in my youth—the families of schoolmates I envied, for my view on Amsterdam Avenue was a clutter of warehouses and buildings crisscrossed with fire escapes, and a clatter of tracks. Nice people live there still, for the exposure of the Drive, the brightness and clearness, and the piercing winds of winter are no attraction to the creatures of darkness who infest the side streets in this part of town. Here, on the Drive, are people in love with the river and the sun, at all hours, in all seasons, and who must—by the sheer constant presence of natural forces—be somehow cleansed by them. Even dull and viewless West End Avenue has a spaciousness that allows man to breathe, and an exemption from visible commerce that allows him other thoughts than buying or selling.

As for the brownstones—street after street after street of them, running from River to Park—they once provided, as do certain streets in European cities, the peace of monotony, the pattern of stability. But here is the greatest change of all in thirty-five years. These houses, tenanted each by one family, polished and scoured by maids, the glass of the windows bright, spelled safety. An apartment-house child like myself looked upon them with a certain wistfulness: it was exciting—a privilege—to visit a girl in one of them. The long flights of stairs, the red-damask walls, and the globe lamps were like a

The West Seventies

17

theater, and there were corners for hiding games and escape from parents.

Now these same brownstones have an evil look, singly and corporately. Nearly all of them have become rooming houses, run by landlords who preside over their decay. So many of the windows are gray with grime, their yellow shades dirty and torn, so many of the stoops and cornices are crumbled, that the single clean window with flower boxes is a gesture of courage and gallantry, and the single painted façade a constant reproach to surrounding sloth and neglect.

"Nice" people still live in these brownstones— many of them refugees of the late 1930's, German and Austrian Jews who are psychiatrists, scholars, musicians, teachers, artisans, unable to afford living elsewhere; together with a number of American professionals, they form islands of decency in a brown sea of squalor. For greater poverty has moved in next to them: Puerto Ricans crowded ten in a room, spilling over the stoops into the streets, forced through no fault of their own to camp indoors as well as out, warming their souls on the television set and blanking out thought with the full volume of radio. And for every mother who keeps her bare room tidy and her children spotless, there are those who shuffle, pregnant, with five children, to market; their long hair matted, their high heels worn, gaudy in magenta. And for every clean and cheerful and diligent delivery boy or proficient and pretty manicurist, there are the sullen boys with pomaded ducktails and the tough girls with scorn-

The New York I Know

ful eyes, hanging around the stoops, chattering roughly. Although the Puerto Ricans are no tougher or rougher, no more sullen or scornful than native New York equivalents here and elsewhere, they have taken over, without will or design but merely by numbers and poverty, those parts of the city doomed by avarice and abandonment to be slums. Their only sin lies in their majority: they outnumber their white neighbors-in-squalor—the perverts, addicts, delinquents, criminals, and failures who infest the city.

Thirty years ago there were mad people and bad people in those brownstones too. But their insanity and sin were private then; they did not invade the street, fouling the public air and affronting the eye.

Sometimes, on a very cold and brilliant winter day, when the windows of all the brownstones are closed and the street is empty of people, a row of them in one of the "better" streets can still revive some illusion of their past, some vision of order, however melancholy. But in summer the sores are open and the infection visible.

And the avenues—Broadway, Amsterdam, and Columbus—what of them? They had then, as they have now, the faceless, planless ugliness of all American cities. But it is no exercise in nostalgia to say that the ugliness then was clean and cheerful— an amiable hodgepodge of low buildings along wide streets—while now it is for the most part sordid and littered, a shoddy monument to quick growth and quicker senescence. Broadway in its upper reaches has a sort of bustling brashness, and in summer

The New York I Know

20

there is a certain pathos in the little concrete islands between traffic where old people and tired people sit with their faces lifted to the sun, numb to the enveloping roar of truck and bus. They are too old and too tired to walk west to the River or east to the Park; and it is a testament to the brutality of our cities that this is all they have.

As for the rich and favored—and the West Side still has its share—they live in the big apartment buildings that face Central Park, from the low Sixties to the high Eighties. It is only a line one building thick that separates them from the rotting brownstones and the rotting poor, with the exception of Seventy-second, Seventy-seventh, and Eighty-first Streets, where the line is one block thick. To live in these places is not as expensive as in their Fifth Avenue counterparts across the trees and lakes, but it is far from cheap and is costing more yearly. The apartments are large and usually well maintained, and only the doormen are apt to reflect the inferior social geography: they are neither as arrogant nor as efficient as their East Side brothers.

But West Side richness is different from East Side wealth, not only because it is predominantly Jewish, derived in large part from the dress business and show business, but because the women dress conspicuously for show. Nowhere is their ostentation more visible than in the beauty salon where they—and I—go for our hair.

Take Mrs. Stein, the wife of a lining manufacturer. She changes the color of her hair every three

The New York I Know

22

months. In this last year she has been platinum mauve, strawberry blonde, and auburn red, and she has now expressed a nostalgia for her own color: "Maybe it's softer?" She spends at least nine hours a week in the salon, and I have never seen her in the same dress, although each dress is similarly tight over hips and bust. In the middle of a weekday she wears all her jewelry—four heavy gold bracelets, a diamond watch, a diamond ring the size of an acorn, pearls, pearl and diamond earrings, and two gold and diamond clips. Like many of the other ladies, Mrs. Stein goes in heavily for plastic, especially in summer: transparent plastic handbags and plastic mules with very high heels. Her mink stoles are extra long, her mink coats are extra dark, and whenever she has a party ahead she has her hair set specially for it, usually in the most extreme current style. Her rather battered face is now framed by a wide solid puff of auburn, high on the head.

Or take Shirley, as they call her there. Shirley is as beautiful as a show girl. In fact, she was one until her more permanent establishment as the friend of an East Side gentleman in a West Side flat. She is far smarter than Mrs. Stein, but she too dresses daily as others might dress for cocktails, wearing her treasures.

Some of the ladies, on the other hand, live in the hotel in which the salon is situated, and they appear in tight toreador pants, sweaters, and flats, not emerging from their apartments until evening. But their conversation is of yachts in Florida, cruises in winter, and fun at the Concord.

The West Seventies

23

Two years ago all the local ladies carried *Exodus* under their arms. Last year it was *Advise and Consent*. But their main preoccupations are weight, television stars, dress, and food. Yet, according to the girl who does her nails, Mrs. Stein "is a doll—got a heart of gold." And a lot of the others must be like her.

The rich spend as little time as they can west of Central Park where they live, for the pattern of their lives is either to go east for fashion and food or south for business and pleasure. They cannot be blamed for this, because there are only two attractions a westward stroll can offer (except for the River, and who walks there?). One is pastries and one is delicatessen, and the best of both are here in profusion. In one block alone are seven pastry shops, all good; within two blocks, six delicatessens, one with the best smoked salmon in the city.

Yet while there are twenty-seven bars in a ten-block area of two avenues, there is not one really good bookshop, and the florists are few and mean. The woman in search of good wholesome provender in vegetables and fruits must choose between one stand six long blocks away or a series of groceries offering produce so flabby and wilted that it is one small remove from garbage. The sophistication of East Side food shelves are only now beginning to reach the West Side. The few stores that stock imported delicacies and the less usual fruits and greens are either too far for easy shopping, or too expensive for the average purse. On the West Side, money cannot buy any of the many small

pleasures that make daily living a pleasure; it can buy only escape.

Thus the successful men can escape to business, and the successful women can remain in their comfortable rooms overlooking the Park and telephone for what they need, avoiding contact wherever possible with their environment and their neighbors.

But while this may keep them safe and uncontaminated, they are divorcing themselves from a truth that concerns them urgently: a pocket of cancer threatens every healthy cell of blocks. One short walk daily, in summer and winter, would tell them all they needed to know of a corrupt, diseased, and self-destroying town.

So come with me—preferably on some clement morning—from Central Park West on Seventy-second, heading west. It is a broad street, flanked on both sides—except for a parking lot on one—by tall apartment buildings, of which the Dakota is the oldest and the most distinguished, and by apartment hotels with faintly baronial Anglo-Saxon names. The masculine residents of these hotels are not on the street in daytime, not even—except in very warm weather—the few old men. One suspects, in fact, that the great majority of their inhabitants are elderly women. They are everywhere visible: those over thirty in mink, those over fifty in black Persian lamb, their hair at all ages fresh from the hairdresser and usually ash blonde, their faces carefully tinted, their bags expensive. With the older women especially you get the feeling that their sons have been good to Mama, setting her up in a nice

The New York I Know

26

hotel, and giving her the best of everything except their presence. For this is a lonely race of women without husbands or family, passing their time with cards and television and charities, or in the beauty salon. If you stripped them of their furs, their tints, and their cosmetics, they would be the old gossips on the streets of Odessa or Tel Aviv, but they would be real and their faces would not be masks of emptiness. Yet perhaps these ladies on this particular street are the lucky ones, for at the hairdresser you hear the refrain over and over again: "They had to put her away; she couldn't remember anything."

Between the hotels and Columbus Avenue there is a brief strip of commerce: a newsdealer and candy shop, a cleaner's, a tailor's, a furrier's, a delicatessen and a hamburger bar, exhaling a greasy breath. Turn left, then, on Columbus, a broad avenue with truck-filled traffic thundering one way south like a herd of bison. On this corner is a newsstand presided over by a fat woman with cold black eyes and containing—besides the usual mass magazines, papers, and comics—Spanish, Jewish, German, and Russian periodicals, and a copious display of pornography ranging from the sophisticated slicks to small butcher-paper magazines devoted to violence, sadism, perversion, and just plain smut. This is a standard assortment of the district, well patronized.

There is nothing unusual about this particular block as you turn left—a drugstore, a delicatessen, a lingerie shop, a candy and comics parlor, a grocer, two bars—but the people on it reveal its temper and

The New York I Know

28

style. You may see, for instance, a thin girl in tight pants, her pale face free of makeup except for eye black, and her hair arranged in loose and stringy Bardot fashion. She is carrying a bundle of wash to the laundromat, eying and eyed by two boys with pompadour cuts and short leather jackets. She might be an unemployed television actress or, simply, a slut.

In the dark interior of the bar with an Irish name, at an early afternoon hour, sit four men, drinking but not speaking. Their heads turn to see a woman stumble out into the street. She is middle-aged, her face is puffy, her thin hair matted, and her stockings wrinkled above her clumsy shoes as she wanders uncertainly down the street. She is seeing nothing and going nowhere, but she knows enough to wait for the lights before crossing the avenue.

A Negro girl with bright-red hair and defiant mouth and eyes comes out of a squalid hotel across the street and walks south slowly and provocatively, her breasts sharp in a tight jersey, her small buttocks moving in tight pants. As she passes the open door of the bar, the men inside look and snigger, but her eyes are where her thoughts are, and who knows them? But she knows the thoughts of others as she walks by.

Three youths in dungarees walk north, and even a half block away their walk is unnatural. As they come close you can see that all three have painted lips, that one wears marcelled hair in a bob and a long string of beads, that another has false breasts under his shirt, and that the third, a Negro, has a

29

31

boxer's build and a dancer's gait. As they walk they talk in high exaggerated lisping speech, uttering short obscenities and laughing at them. Some of the people they pass laugh back at them, but most draw away, revulsion in their eyes, as they step aside to let the profane and hideous trio pass.

When you reach Seventy-first Street and before you cross it, you notice the old man leaning against a corner railing there: his perch. Long and gangling, with his wide felt hat and toothless grinning face, he looks like an ancient hillbilly gone to seed. Sometimes he babbles to friends from the neighboring bar, sometimes he does a little jig on the pavement and sings a cracked and jumbled tune. It is hard to tell how foolish he is: there is something in his eyes that betrays knowledge; of men, of animals, of descent. In all these he finds humor.

On the next block, nothing will catch your eye (used as it is to the encompassing decay) but a marvelous stand of vegetables—the freshest, the biggest, the shiniest peas and tomatoes and eggplants and parsley and lettuce and spinach and carrots you ever saw. Sitting watching them is a white-haired man in a white coat, and he watches them with positive love, sprinkling them with water on hot days, arranging them so that no fruit bruises another and no vegetable is without air. If you are innocent and ask him how much are the peas, he will say in a strong foreign accent, "Fifty cents a pound," and you say, incredulously, "Fifty cents a pound?" or "I'm afraid that's too high," and he will turn on you and heap abuse and tell you he doesn't want you as a customer if you can't tell a good pea from a bad one, to go away and leave him alone. "Crazy," says the florist next door. But the old abusive man and his beautiful greens adorn that block.

Turn left then at the end of the block, and walk east by the brownstones. It is a typical street of rooming houses, some with "Vacancy" signs, some with signs saying "Vedanta Society" or "World Theosophy" or "Yoga," for the West Side is full of ways to attain other levels, whether through hypnotism—"The New York Center of Hypnotism" is two blocks north—or through the attentions of a "Reader and Advisor"—a gypsy or Puerto Rican woman who divines destiny through cards or stars.

On the top floor of one brownstone live two young women secretaries, sharing a two-room flat. They had lived there for some months, they said, before they realized that their landlord preferred to rent to homosexuals like himself and that they were the only women in the house. Their neighbors, in fact, were three young men, neat and well-mannered, who lent and borrowed sugar or lemons or soda as good neighbors will. The only disquieting element in their proximity was the occasional content of their trash baskets set out for the night: women's hats, blouses, and accessories.

But what proved infinitely more disturbing to the two young women was their daily view from their windows on the street. They could not look out without seeing through the window of the ground floor room of the brownstone opposite: a window with shades never lowered and curtains never

*The West
Seventies*

drawn, lit brightly at night. Directly below the window was a bed and on the bed, no matter what time they looked, a young man sprawled and awake, sometimes alone, sometimes with another youth. Finally they could not bear to look at all, drawing their blinds and shutting out the street. An older resident of the neighborhood tried to reassure them: "It goes on all over here," he said. "The place is full of bums and perverts who never work, who live on God knows what, and who want to be seen. Just forget about it."

What he might have added was that the place was also full of decent people who worked and were not seen, except in their places of business. There is, for instance, Mort the cleaner who takes in dirty clothes from eight in the morning until seven at night six days a week and never fails to smile as he notes them down. There are Mr. and Mrs. Kruger who are experts in Elizabethan music, their musty apartment full of the lovely round-bellied, slim-waisted instruments that used to delight the first great queen. There is Mrs. Shapiro the dressmaker who spent five years in Dachau and Belsen and whose children are buoyant Americans. There is the distinguished aging actor with his hair long on his collar who takes his spaniel for a daily run in the park. There is Mrs. Kleinerman who runs a delicatessen store with her husband and says, "If I had a brain I would die happy." There is the old porter Mike who goes home each night to eight parakeets, the goal of all his days.

The West Side is full of people like that, who do

34

not walk the streets and parade their afflictions of mind and soul. They spend as little time outside the small harbors of their homes and offices as they can, shutting out the continuous small brutalities of the neighboring world and keeping their children off the streets after six at night. And among themselves, and when they meet strangers from out of town or abroad, they say: "The neighborhood gets worse every day, but what can you do? Maybe Lincoln Square will clean up some of the dirt."

The West Seventies

35

2. *Central Park*

CENTRAL PARK is many things. It is the calm eye in the center of a hurricane. It is the vision of men who knew man's needs. It is the measure of seasons in a city which tries to insulate itself from them. It is the refuge of wild things escaping stone. It is a zone of danger. It is the only sleeping land in a sleepless city. And it is the only place, aside from the Jersey and Brooklyn shores and the Upper Bay, from which the dream of Manhattan is wholly visible because the eye has room to embrace it and the heart the distance to love it.

Central Park is also the view from my window; standing close, that is. For lying on my bed I see only a wide pane of sky crossed intermittently by the plunge of pigeons or—much farther off and much higher—by the slow, supremely easy arc of gulls as they ride on thermal currents. They are dirty rapacious birds, but distance divests them of squalor.

Directly below my window is the bridle path, and beyond that a triangle of trees and grass where the neighborhood dogs run free, and beyond that the pompous stone back of Daniel Webster, one of the strange assortment of statues—Shakespeare, Morse, Humboldt, Mazzini—which nobody looks at. But the focal point of the view is the double lake: two winding irregular ponds, the narrow waist between them spanned by a delicate iron bridge, very gently arched and persistently Japanese in feeling, especially when a small figure stands on the curve, reflected by still water below, and especially on misty afternoons.

Beyond the lake and the boathouse, the Metropolitan Museum to the northeast and the bandstand shell to the southeast, are the apartments of Fifth Avenue—the windows and terraces and water towers and penthouses ranged behind a mile of trees like a line of rich relatives, sober and correct, marshaled by the taller Carlyle tower behind them. But they too can be transformed, not by distance so much as by light. For when a clear sun sets in early fall and winter they are washed in an apricot glow, their windows inflamed and brilliant, and then they might be some desert city of palaces. So beautiful are they, behind dark trees and against a darkening sky, that no matter where I am in the city at that hour, I am impelled to rush home and stare at them before the sun is down and the grayness takes over.

And if I crane my neck and face south, I see even greater splendor: the cluster of stalagmites south of Fifty-ninth Street, a pattern of older spires and newer slabs so magnificent in their soaring arrangement that the accident which is Manhattan seems a deliberate creative act.

When is the Park most beautiful from my window? In heavy snow, I think; or the pale green fuzzing of early spring. When the snow has stopped falling and is still blindingly white, and the lake is frozen, the rough ice sparsely dotted with skating

38

and slipping black figures, and the branches are black, then Breughel comes alive. And all the dogs, leaping and racing black silhouettes, are delirious in the snow. Later, after the interminable dead brown sleep of winter, after snow, the first faint blurring of the trees is an excitement. And still later, when the lake is alive with colored boats and rowing people, distance again bestows an innocence on this popular pleasure which closer attention might dispel: the rowdies shout four-letter words as they ram a stranger, and fat men with cigars throw bottles in the lake.

There is a certain lushness about full summer: the heavy denseness of green over all, the leaves unstirred by wind, the whole Park breathing like a tired beast. In the intolerable heat of July, the small white naked bodies of boys splash in the fringes of the lake and climb on rocks, and somehow I think of Thomas Eakins.

But summer stirs the beast too, for this is the time of danger when human animals hide in the cover of leaves and darkness. And even from my room, high up above, I can hear on a stifling night cries which might be horseplay but which could also be screams of fear. Indeed, I once heard a woman cry "Help! Help!," and I rushed to the window at midnight but saw nothing except the lamplight shining through the heavy trees and the rest in blackness.

But let us, as they used to say in television, zoom in closer; using, however, different lenses, for the Park must be seen through different kinds of eyes if we are to know it fully. There is the eye of the child,

Central Park

39

the eye of the mother and nurse, the eye of the walker and watcher, and each is different.

I don't know how much the eye of a child has changed since I was small—I suspect that a profusion of secondhand marvels has reduced the capacity for delight in firsthand ones—but to the very young, the granite boulders in the Park must still be peaks for conquering and a thicket of firs an ambush beckoning courage. Certainly, where I was scaling these slabs, today's children have sculpture—Hans Christian Andersen and his duck, or the too-elaborate Alice in Wonderland tea party—to crawl over. And where I clung proudly to my wooden carrousel horse, feeling (I know now) that wonderful sense of pride which a real horse gives his rider, the kids are now gliding up and down on theirs with the same proud glee in their eye: "Look at me! Look at me!"

But some things have changed. The infants and toddlers of the rich still go to the Park with their mothers and nurses, although most of them seek playgrounds rather than the natural contours of hill and rock: "The ground is filthy," said one young mother, "broken glass in the grass, and heaven knows what in the bushes." And on the east side of the Park especially, a caste system is clearly discernible and closely adhered to: *this* playground for mothers with their children, *that* playground for nurses and their charges. Among the nurses, the stratification becomes even more rigid, with the dying breed of nanny at the top and the colored-girl nursemaids at the bottom. Clustered together with

Central Park

their immaculate charges, the middle-aged Swiss, French-Swiss, German, and English nannies exchange their elaborate disdains for the incompetency of their employers. This martyrdom is a part of their superiority and of the basic emotional inadequacies which made them choose their career in the first place. Mothers are thorns in their sides because they themselves are not mothers; yet only they, the nurses, care correctly for children. In a corner, together, the colored maids huddle, miserable in cold weather, far less professional about their charges in any weather. In between these class extremes, the Irish nurses compare their infants and savor their household troubles in a heavy brogue.

But I see very few of the "better-class" children playing in the Park now; partly, I imagine, because of anticipated dangers and partly because the lives of today's well-to-do young are so organized that no time is left for the idle stroll or the desultory games of imagination. It is the misfits, the truants, the ne'er-do-wells who idle and stroll, out of emptiness or an obscure urge toward trouble. Only a heavy fall of snow brings out the well-to-do children and their sleds, and I feel that even here most of them wait for their country weekends or their long country holidays. Decades ago it was not so: the hills were full of friends, shouting and pink-faced; and if you dragged your sled to certain specific knolls, you knew who'd be there.

Skating, too, is a different matter. Then there was no Wollman rink, and we skated only on the lakes when they froze over. Rough or smooth, they were

wonderful: all the space in the world and no need for Muzak; the head sang with joy while the ears rang with cold. No need to go round and round in one direction, no confinement of the experts to one small circle. In the long fingers and coves of the lakes each could take his pace and attempt his curves without the risk—except for the immortal and inescapable show-off, churning the ice in a swathe—of collision. These were the great freedoms of the Park in winter, a resort five blocks away.

I do not remember the Park zoo as a child; we went to the Bronx for our animals. Later, much later, I took my own child to the little zoo by the Arsenal, as most mothers do. But my real pleasure in it is part of a present ritual as a stroller: a point in the diagonal walk from the West Side to the shopping and business Fifties and Fifth Avenue.

A long watch at the sea lions' pool is imperative. There is a large one, who looks male, and two smaller ones, who look female: these two have something clinging and tender about them as they suffer his ill temper. Often I have seen one of them rub up against his fat and shining flank only to get an irritable shrug, a sharp bark in the face, and an edging away. I watch them as they stretch and doze when their bellies are full, and I watch them in their ludicrous anxiety for the midday fish: a constant craning of necks toward the keeper's expected approach, a constant leaping out of water and peering through the railings, blowing a fishy breath, barking and bristling. But I love them best when they are simply playing: performing an underwater ballet so

The New York I Know

44

swift and graceful and full of humor (they race below belly upward, their flippers folded over, then shoot out of water with silly bravura faces) that no sense of captivity remains. They are the only animals there that do not make me actively sad. I cannot bear to look at the big cats—lions, tigers, leopards, cheetahs—because of their hopeless constriction, forced either to doze with their beautiful yellow eyes open or to pace in padded silence all day long. Nor can I find any amusement, as I used to, in the big apes. The look in the eyes of the gorilla frightens me; it is full of an implacable race hatred.

There is a yak there, too, from whom I must turn away. He has a distorted horn that curves up under his chin and he must know his distortion, for he usually stands in a dark corner of his cell, a big black shaggy heap of depression. And I am embarrassed for the moulting camel.

But the Barbary wild sheep fascinate me. They stand in absolute stillness on small rocks to which their hooves seem fastened, while their big goat eyes, full of amber interior light, see nothing. And when there is a baby llama or a baby Sika deer or tahr, I am enchanted by their tentative necks, their long lashes, and their feeble legs, so easily buckled. Theirs is a vulnerability which even our smallest Park children seem to lack.

Central Park

For I watch their faces too, as they come, singly with parents, or in long queues with teachers, to look at the animals, and there is a toughness in too many of them. Their amusement at the animals is contemptuous, and I keep wondering whether any-

45

body has given them a sense of reverence for the multiple marvels of species, for the separate identities of these beasts. Pity, certainly, is an alien emotion to the young. But what of wonder?

The real lovers of the zoo by the Arsenal appear to be foreigners. German, Russian, Italian, French, Czech—the chatter at the tables of the cafeteria and at the benches facing the sea-lion pool is all of these. In fact, it is the foreigners who walk in any weather, finding in the Park some answer to their craving for peace in a city that provides no islands of rest or simple sociability in its midst.

It is a source of deep amazement to me that the Park is so little used by the people of the city, except as an escape from heat in summer. For nine months of the year it is virtually empty during the day except for the playgrounds and on holidays. On glorious days of sun and wind or of soft grayness I have crossed the Park time and again and met no more than five others on the way. It is this very loneliness now that makes me walk by the main arteries rather than on the smaller paths; even in daylight I cannot rule out the thought of danger.

But why, in a city of eight million, are there not more who feel the need of sky overhead and earth underneath? who must stretch legs in a long stride and the chest with a long breath? They cannot all be day workers. Are American legs really so atrophied? There is pleasure even in watching those common animals the squirrels. Their tails fold so neatly over their backs, their paws are so expert holding nuts. And there is always this question: Do

The New York I Know

46

they remember where they buried their own nuts, or do they dig up somebody else's? I am constantly diverted, too, by the foolishness of dogs who strain at the leash in whimpering yearning to chase them. Or who, unleashed, race after squirrels and end at the foot of trees looking upwards, quivering.

And I cannot see one of these respectable rodents without remembering a fire that took place last year in a hollow tree on the edge of the Park near by. Firemen came to put it out, and when an elderly woman observer asked one of the hosemen, "What is it, officer, what happened?," he turned to her with a face empty of guile and said, "Squirrel—smoked in bed."

And what of the birds? Early on a spring morning I have looked out of my window and seen a little band of people across the lake, their elbows raised as they hold binoculars up. They are bird watchers, of course, and a happier company never was, for they live on hope interspersed with shocks of joy: there he is, the first hermit thrush!—or the first rose-breasted grosbeak!—or the first magnolia warbler! And after this hour they can go to their offices or their homes with a sense of buoyant completion denied their fellows. I am neither knowledgeable nor dedicated enough to be of their kind, but even I find joy in the flight of strange birds and a call I never heard before. And some mornings, without stirring from my room, I can hear the first morning song—strangely like distant sleighbells— of the feathered population of the Park. There is solace in this irrepressible, inalterable act of nature

The New York I Know

48

in the midst of gigantic artifice.

Still another dedicated group are the model-boat sailors on the round pond at Seventy-second Street. Their miniature yachts, perfect with mahogany and brass, intricate rigging, and the right pennants, are products of great love and years of hours. And when they take the wind, lean over, and race toward the other lip of the pool leaving a miniature hissing wake, the eyes of their owners—hurrying to meet them—are no less solicitous than a parent's.

All these people, in fact: the people who love birds, the people who love dogs, the old chess players in their little stone pagoda, the bowlers on their greens, the expert horsemen and horsewomen— these are the best citizens of this realm of the Park simply because they love. It is those sick with lack of love or interest who harm. Even the old shabby woman with her paper bag full of crumbs for the pigeons who need none is better than they, sick though she may be too for want of love.

In summer, of course, music and drama will bring people to the Park. And although spoiled like most New Yorkers by a wealth of both on easier terms, and averse to crowds, I have gone on a suffocating night to look and hear. The reward is less in the per- formance (the music is pedestrian, though the act- ing in Joseph Papp's Shakespeare can be of high quality) than in the faces of those who listen: a rapt intentness that brings out the best of men and women for they are losing themselves in something beyond them. The old look less tired, and the young, in attitudes of love on the grass, more tender.

The New York
I Know

50

But on the fringes of the innocent, the evil gather. Heat and night bring the roaches from their crevices, and then the Park becomes a jungle. (Even in my childhood there was danger: our doctor arrived one evening bruised and cut from an assault by two thugs who took his watch and money. And in broad daylight two things happened which I cannot forget. Once a man with his features obliterated by blood came out of a thicket, staggering, and I fled in terror. And once, in deep winter, in the same rambles which the prudent now avoid, I came upon a man in an act which I did not understand but which wholly revolted me. I ran, sickened, the half mile to my home.)

Now, of course, there is more violence and more perversity. The Park has become not only a stalking ground for young predators and rapists; it is a point of assignation for homosexuals, and I need go no further than my window to see the figure of a man waiting behind a tree and later joined by another man, who walks with him under the heavy shadows of leaves and out of sight. And a walk down to Fifty-ninth Street on the western verge of the Park some steaming day is a line-up (or lie-down) of derelicts, some sleeping on benches or grass, others muttering to themselves, others sitting in a hopeless stupor of alcohol. They are there, to be sure, not for an evil purpose, but because even in their befuddlement the Park is kinder than the grimy furnished rooms where they live, and the dirty grass cooler than their beds.

And the police? They rove the main roads period-

The New York I Know

52

ically in patrol cars, and I have seen two give summonses to women for letting small dogs off the leash in an area devoid of people. But in my walks across the Park, there are days when I meet no patrolman.

When Central Park first came into being over a hundred years ago, its architects saw it as a refuge for the well rather than an asylum for the sick. Frederick Law Olmsted and Calvert Vaux, who landscaped this great tract of featureless land spotted with shanties, saw it for what it was: the salvation of the city, the delight of the citizen. They had a mayor, Ambrose C. Kingsland, who furthered their aim, and a board of commissioners distinguished by the presence of William Cullen Bryant, who edited the New York *Evening Post* from 1829 to 1878, and Andrew Jackson Downing, who edited the *Horticulturist*. For five years these men and others fought for this central site, and for five and a half million dollars it was finally bought from its private owners by the city. A triumph over the "practical" rapacity of real-estate interests who wept at the waste of building sites, Central Park became the first park in the United States, and a model for most that followed.

But now Vaux and Olmsted and Downing and Bryant would weep at the Park they made, not if they looked at it from my window but if they walked its paths as I do and looked closely. Everywhere they would see the contempt and negligence of man: the litter of cellophane and bottletops in the bottom of every grove; the jumble of paper cups and containers and cans and bottles at the fringe of

Central Park

53

once-clear lakes; the newspapers left lying on the grass, to blow, get sodden, and stick among the twigs; the accumulated dust of city and man that spreads a gray dry film over the freshness of growth, exhausting before its time.

Some of it, in the middle of a giant city, is inescapable. Much of it is the fault of municipal poverty, alloting a handful of workers where battalions are needed to keep the land from eroding, the trees from dying, and the grass from despoliation. But most of the fault lies with the people for whom the Park was made, or rather for the generations that succeeded them. Undisciplined barbarians have done this to the Park, as if to vent on nature what they cannot on stone. Without pride, without love, without innocence, they use this public bounty for their private ends, ravishing and wrecking as they go. Even the rats have taken heart from this. They now crawl openly in daylight along the bridle path, scavenging.

Against this ravishment, the Central Park Association and men like Robert Moses have done what they can, which they know is not enough. And generous citizens have endowed boathouses, fountains, and gardens to keep the idea of natural pleasures alive. To them we owe what small beauties are left. As to the larger ones, nothing can spoil the wide sweep of the sheep meadow spread before the great southern towers of Manhattan. Nothing can spoil the brilliant rippled rectangle of the Reservoir. Nothing can spoil what you see when you look from a window high on the southern border of the

The New York I Know

56

Park: miles and miles of trees and clearings which seem to lead not to Harlem, which is invisible, but to freedom.

The Park contains the unconquerable forces of life itself, which persists in flowering, persists in enduring, and still states, every spring, with an explosion of purpose, its essential immortality.

3. *Park Avenue*

IF YOU ARE VERY RICH and want the best that New York can offer, you will be likely to live in one of several places and several ways, all of them in one rectangle of Manhattan's gridiron bounded roughly by Central Park and the East River, between the Fifties or Sixties, where commerce prevails, to Ninety-sixth Street, where slums take over.

You will have a high apartment on Fifth Avenue looking over Central Park toward a range of buildings whose outlines in no way suggest inferior status and seem, in fact, just as desirable as your own. Or you will buy a brownstone on a quiet side street lined with trees, and remodel it to your taste; or—if you can get it—one of the lovely Georgian-style houses on Sutton Place which front on dead-end streets and conceal, behind them, rolling and flowering lawns that reach to the East River. Or, loving the life of the river with its fretwork of bridges and the ever-absorbing glide of tugs and barges and freighters on its oily current, yet preferring height, you will rent or buy an apartment or penthouse in one of the new white buildings where your balcony becomes a liner's prow, with only water below; where the opalescent ribbon of the river winds south or north changing consistency and tone with every hour; and where, at night, the flow of cars on the East River Drive is another winking river of lights, mesmeric and silent.

If you are not so rich and can't afford such conspicuous beauties and privileges, you will still pay dearly for the social and business prestige which a "good" address confers, for easy access to the best doctors and psychiatrists, and to the best shops, whether they are big and sell clothes or little and sell everything from Syrian coffee to Caspian caviar, from Burmese silk to Dresden china, from collages to sporting prints.

You will pay $500 a month for a four-room apartment built like a filing cabinet on streets where cars can barely crawl and where people who live below the tenth floor can see nothing but stone and windows. But you will also be paying for the fact that this is the first section of the city to be cleared of snow after a blizzard and of garbage after a strike, and that the double-parked limousines of its residents are the last to be ticketed. They are, in fact, not ticketed at all. Privilege is the password, policed and bribed.

You pay for other things too. The men and women who walk along Fifth and Madison and Park and Lexington and now even Third are more smartly dressed than the citizens of other neighborhoods, and it is possible to see the assured bearing and the kind of well-bred face, with fine bones and clear skin now increasingly rare in any of our cities. If the women wear minks, tweeds are underneath them, and they walk in simple pumps with low

The New York I Know

heels. On these East Side streets you are not likely to find men in vicuña coats spitting on the sidewalk or women in Dior dresses chewing gum.

Even the dogs are conscious of their breeding: the big black poodles sit bolt upright in the seat next to the chauffeur, like witty French countesses off to the races, their tufted chins tilted above their rhinestone collars, their eyes beady, their topknots fresh from the drier. Even the tiny topiary toys seem fluffier and more impertinent on the East Side; their mistresses no more infatuated but more likely to reveal, in their doting faces, the puffiness of martinis and self-pampering.

It is because you want such things, some tangible like a view, some intangible like prestige, that you pay to live in this congested rectangle. The abiding mystery of the fashionable East Side, however, is the deliberate choice of residence on Park Avenue, the most boring street of its kind for its entire residential length.

From Sixtieth to Ninety-sixth Street, opposing cliffs of apartment houses face each other over a river of traffic and a dividing line of meager rectangles which roof the New York Central tracks. Because most of these apartments were built forty years ago when architecture was bogged down in sterile pretentious conservatism, the view from any living-room window is ranks of small windows meanly spaced in façades of gray or dun stone undistinguished either by handsome proportions or good decorative detail. Below, the yellow cabs and the black Cadillacs stream past these graceless

Park Avenue

plots of tired privet, dusty grass, and iron railing, only sometimes relieved by lighted Christmas trees or clumps of spring or autumn flowers donated by a benefactress and sturdy enough to survive a fortnight of fumes. For this, and for an address that implies position and wealth, thousands of New Yorkers pay prodigious rents, willing to starve their eyes and congest their lungs for the security of status.

It is all the more remarkable that people of taste and no thirst for status can be found on Park Avenue, and they will probably depreciate the address and say that the rooms are large and the location handy. From the back windows, too, provided they are high up, glimpses of roofs and river give some idea of the city's superior beauties. But even these escape hatches and the penthouses with their full-grown trees and shrubs cannot be reached without the subtle penance of a Park Avenue entrance: the apotheosis of a kind of stuffiness, of a social self-consciousness, that few free spirits could face every day and night without distaste.

The Park Avenue lobby would, in fact, give pause to excavators of the future, should they find one intact and furnished. For although their shape and their contents vary widely—some are Regency, some Renaissance, some French provincial or Jacobean, some contemporary (even to subdued abstractions and wire sculpture), they share the same muffled discretion, the same soft sell: you who enter here are in the right place with the right people. Supporting this message, of course, are the door-

62

men, a very special breed. The better ones are courteous and helpful, but like headwaiters or jewelry salesmen or art dealers, their duty is appraisal. They do not look: they size up. For strangers, their gaze is a gantlet. And to the imaginative, their flicker of acceptance is as disturbing as tacit rejection. Only the insecure find pleasure in being considered acceptable.

If the lobby is a form of insulation from the living world outside, an even greater one is the street itself. For Park Avenue is an estrangement from the realities of New York, of which two are the most valuable: the peculiar haphazard beauty of the city, and its structure of villages.

This structure is basically triangular, and consists of the relation of side street to avenue, of residence to commerce, of privacy to common experience. Every avenue on the East Side has this corner life except Park Avenue (Fifth at least has a people's park), for the tributaries are residential like the main stream, and the purpose for walking is to exercise the dog or go to church on Sundays. To live in the side streets near Lexington or Third or Second, on the other hand, is to be part of an intimate complex of people and services that form, as time goes on, a close familiar whole in the midst of the great fragmentation which is the city. At no time are you more than a half block away from butcher, grocer, stationer, liquor dealer, cleaner, or florist, with each of whom daily contact becomes friendship as well as habit. And on every block or two there is that dim little shabby Irish bar, more haven than hang-

The New York I Know

64

out. The big new developments obliterate more of these villages every year, substituting impersonal order for intimate confusion, but where they still cling they give New York its heart.

Park Avenue has no such beat. Few women (one hesitates to call them housewives) can be bothered often with a two-block walk, nor need they be with the telephone at hand and servants dispatchable for errands. When they leave their apartments they go to those of friends or the shops in the Fifties, confining their local excursions to a fancy grocery on Madison Avenue (to pick up some Spanish artichoke hearts) or to a place where Quiche Lorraine is made for parties. And their husbands, with the Racquet Club or "21" handier, are not likely to take in a Third Avenue bar on their homeward trip.

Park Avenue, then, is an island. But who are the islanders? What manner of people choose this isolation? Solvency is no answer, for the rich have better alternatives. Nor is success in business or profession the determinant. Park Avenue is full of successful people, but so are the side streets. In earlier days origins played a part, but now the proportion of Jews and Gentiles is roughly equal, even though some co-operatives manage a policy of exclusion without stating it. Café society and *Social Register* society are broadly represented, philanthropists abound, and few buildings fail to include at least one member of that tenacious and long-lived little company—the only refugees blessed by society— the White Russians.

Park Avenue   But there are other people, too, on Park Avenue.

65

Take the young Petersons, who inherited their apartment from his family. They hate the Avenue, but where else could they afford to keep their five children on his salary as an editor in a publishing house? Or take Dr. Kuhn, the famous urologist. His office is in the building, his life is his work, and think of the time he saves. Or take old Mrs. Worthington. She has lived in the same apartment for thirty-five years, with her two Irish maids and her ten rubber plants and her sixteen ferns: what would she do in another world, where people lived? And then, of course, there are residents like the Haggertys. Clyde Haggerty makes forty thousand a year after taxes as president of his construction firm. It costs him that much to live as he thinks he must live, on Park Avenue, and he will leave nothing when he dies. He is paying for an ice floe that will melt while others are paying for an elaborate ark in a treacherous sea, for safety within danger.

There are many reasons to live on Park Avenue; as many reasons, perhaps, as residents, as many good as bad. Yet if I were asked to describe typical Park Avenue apartments or typical Park Avenue parties, I think I would concentrate on two particular kinds. One would be the home of a *Social Register* kind of family, the other would belong, say, to the president of a chain of department stores.

Let us visit George and Amy Lansing first. George is an investment banker with a Wall Street firm, Amy is the daughter of a prominent corporation lawyer, lately deceased. George's family has lived in Glens Falls for five generations, Amy's an-

The New York I Know

66

cestors fought the Revolution in Virginia. They have a daughter at Brearley, a son at Yale, and a house at Stockbridge, used on weekends and summer vacations. George is on many boards, Amy on many charities. Their large rooms are carpeted wall-to-wall in a neutral shade, the sofas and chairs are covered either in flowered muted chintz or in beige brocade, and the curtains drawn across the windows are of matching chintz. The furniture is mostly English antique. Over the fireplace is a portrait, thinly painted, of Amy's mother—the kind of woman with the long sloping undivided bust mysteriously achieved in her day, and an expression of mild reproof. The other pictures are mostly etchings of ducks in flight or English hunting prints, and the tops of tables are crowded with family photographs in silver frames. There is nothing in the rooms that could possibly offend anyone and nothing that could possibly delight. The Lansings have comfort for their money but no fun, and the observant guest cannot help but pity such spiritual constipation. What is more, two sets of curtains and a half-lowered shade cut out in daytime the luxury of light that their fifteenth-floor apartment could provide them, and this perpetual muffling and diffusion and carpeting and covering gives these rooms the feeling of large and elaborate padded cells in which one could die of anoxia. Physically and mentally, the Lansings are sealed in their own amber.

This is never more apparent than at one of their cocktail parties. For they invite themselves: pleasant, easy, handsome people from the world of

The New York I Know

68

law or finance, usually Republicans, always well-groomed and always well-mannered. In vain is the search for an expressive, unguarded face, or even an ugly one. At the Lansings you will see no Jews, no artists, no musicians, no eccentrics, and only those foreigners—usually from the north of Europe —who could be taken, except for their accents, for Americans or Englishmen of the Lansings' class. No voice is raised here except in joviality, no alien note intrudes, no new thought penetrates to surprise or disturb. The smooth organization of the party is assured by Amy's own pleasant competence and the work of two efficient maids, one attached to the Lansing household, one specially hired for the evening. These maids are an East Side phenomenon, exerting a prissy gentility which even impeccable menservants fail to impose. There is something about such women, pouring drinks or handing hors d'oeuvres around, which, since it suggests prolonged virginity, acts as a vague depressant. All in all, the Lansing living room is the social equivalent of that experiment in weightlessness and the absence of sensory reflexes in which a man is suspended in tepid water: there is nothing to move against or measure against.

The Kappels, a few blocks north, are very different in certain ways. For one thing, Joseph Kappel's grandparents emigrated from Europe in the middle of the nineteenth century and Liz is a born New Yorker of Midwestern stock. For another, Joe *Park* started fairly humbly as a small importer of fabrics *Avenue* and in twenty years amassed a chain of high-class

69

department stores in New York and the suburbs. The Kappels are much richer than the Lansings and much less inhibited about showing it.

In their apartment, they show it chiefly through the taste of a much sought-after Fifty-seventh Street decorator who changes their decor at intervals to keep pace with fashion. Fifteen years ago Robin persuaded the Kappels to go whole hog on French impressionists, and Joe acquired a rather muddy little Renoir head, a weak Bonnard, a Seurat sketch for "La Grande Jatte," a Degas etching (the laundress), and a very blurry Monet. To complement these, Robin bought them the most expensive examples of French provincial he could find in Europe, and keyed the upholstery with infinite subtlety to their tones.

But last year a revolution took place. Joe took the impressionists to his office (where they impressed), and Robin made over the Kappel home to accommodate a Baziotes, a de Kooning, a Dubuffet, a Franz Kline, and a metal construction composed of pipes and fender strips called "Birdwatcher." All these required white walls, the severest contemporary furniture (including several couches that suggested upholstered mortuary slabs), and the occasional bright jab of an orange, black, or acid-pink pillow. An extra ceiling was suspended, above which invisible fixtures cast diffused light and gave the faces of Kappels and guests the look of recent exhumation. It was quite a room. Only when Liz took women guests to her boudoir did her interior struggle (lost to Robin except in this sanctuary) be-

70

come apparent. An Edzard pastel of a wistful young girl in a ribboned bonnet hung over her frilled and canopied bed, and every white shelf in this pink-lined box was crammed with bibelots: round colored paperweights, white milk glass, and porcelain hands in every position needed to hold nuts, ashes, or a single rose, although never put to these uses.

Although the Kappels have a few close friends from former days to whom they are loyal, and dinners for business associates are given from time to time, their parties are usually reserved for celebrities they know only slightly. Having backed a few Broadway hits, they have access to people of the theater, and Robin has seen to it that the Kappels keep in touch with current newsmakers in the world of art, provided they are socially housebroken. As few of the most prominent contemporary painters qualify, the guests are likely to be museum curators, collectors, critics, and fashion photographers, who give ecstatic sanction to the Kappels' taste but pose no threat to their marriage.

Few would doubt, however, that the Kappel parties were more amusing than the Lansing ones, and the presence of smiling colored barmen adds a festive note that the Lansing maidservants lack. So do contingents of *Vogue* and *Bazaar* models, whose gaunt perfections and bizarre coiffures complement the interior.

It might be said that the major difference between these two family residents of Park Avenue is that the Lansings have roots and the Kappels have none. George and Amy are secure in their past, Joe and Liz are insecure in their present. And while the Lansings accept Park Avenue as a matter of course in their way of living, the Kappels remind themselves of their position every time the doorman greets them.

What they share in common is a dead street in a living city: a street that neither partakes of the splendid conspicuous affluence symbolized by the few private mansions still left nor has a part in the city's tumultuous present and, so far as we can see it, in the radical innovations of the future. Only above Ninety-sixth Street and below Sixtieth Street does Park Avenue come alive: to the north, dangerously and dirtily, with the worst of slums and the greatest of needs; to the south, dynamically and often beautifully, with the transparent thrust of business in the great glass canyon.

Park Avenue Between is an address.

73

4. *The Waterways*

FOUR WATERWAYS embrace Manhattan, each one wholly different from the other, yet all serving to unify that central diversity of stone and human life pointing—like a long crude stake—toward the open sea. From the North River, the Upper Bay, the East River, and the Harlem River, the island has that purity of identity which only distance and the obliteration of the human speck can give it. From the air above, this purity is attained by the shape of the island itself in its girdling water and by the grid pattern that neatly and evenly divides its length and width and by the long green rectangle of park in its central core. You look down on a miracle of aspiration, where man has somehow re-created on a giant scale the crystalline system of matter. Without sight of man himself or the ant which the city reduces him to, the long shadows and shafts and slabs and pinnacles have a permanent and rooted majesty belying accident. Plan is there, but what so excites the spirit from above is the feeling of natural growth, as if this city were inevitable.

So too, yet with more disorder and intimacy, is Manhattan from the rivers and harbor. Or, if you will, from a boat in the waterways, for this is the only way to skirt the island with the detachment that accurate vision demands. From the moment

The Waterways

75

you leave the pier in midtown for the broad strong reaches of the Hudson River, pointing south, the eye, freed from the fragmenting pressure of people and the nagging distractions of detail, opens wide to the fact of Manhattan.

The first fact, of course, is the port. Here lie the giant liners at their berths, their sterns held high, their hulls a swooping trajectory, and their funnels raked with that air of gallantry—like the heads of Directoire dandies—which only ships possess. The red Cunard funnels of the great *Elizabeth,* taller and more restrained in their slant than the low fat tear-drop stacks of the *United States;* the jaunty air of the French ships and—imagination perhaps—a faint whiff of seasoning from the galley; the white-ness and neatness of the Scandinavian vessels—all this nestled along wharves where the pilings are green with moss and the water brown with pollu-tion, shielded from the river current by piers that range from fairly new featureless functionalism backward in time to the piers I knew as a child: green pagoda shapes that the architects of the El stations seemed to fancy, Oriental-municipal and quite incongruous. But they give a feeling neverthe-less of coffee beans and fish and exotic shipments, with no pressures of time, and when they finally crumble I shall be sad.

As you churn down the Hudson you are conscious of the flatness of the city between the high cluster of midtown and the high cluster of downtown, and you remember that this valley of glacial deposit be-tween the rock outcrops is the older city and

The New York I Know

76

Greenwich Village, where low houses still face each other and leave room for sky. And between them and the river are still those warehouses, dark red or old yellow, with blind-bricked windows, that on any waterfront spell the movement of goods and produce, ship chandlers, and the smell of hemp and iron.

On the opposite shore, in Jersey, the letters of commerce are written out more boldly in huge signs: Todd Shipyards, the building for Lipton Tea, with two freighters warped in the pier, the building for Maxwell House Coffee, and suddenly on the wind, the marvelous smell of roasting beans. And only two minutes later the smell of a man shaving (another morning echo) is borne on the breeze from Colgate's Soaps and Perfumes.

Between the trade of Jersey and the luxury shipping of New York the few old ferries still go from shore to shore; dark red or green with their upright virtuous funnels and air of purpose. And always the tugs—four hundred of them work this port—pulling the barges of sand and gravel and freight cars, pushing the giant liners with their matted snouts, breasting the current with that special posture of inpudence which their smallness, their tilt, and their bustle confer on them. By this ceaseless bustle they flaunt their independence of New York, that captive, stationary mammoth.

The widening of the Hudson and the soaring of Manhattan converge, and it is hard to tell which is the more elating: the arrival of destination of a mighty river or the final statement of a mighty city.

The New York I Know

78

You look ahead and the roar and smell of ocean assail you, the wild liberty of three thousand miles of water beyond a statue and an island or two. You look left and you see this pointed massing of stone where the power of man resides: tower behind tower, shaft against shaft, and no conflict between the outmoded fretwork of the Woolworth Building and the white austerity of the new giant Chase Manhattan slab. Even the lower older buildings down on the Battery hold their own, their windows peering seawards under the raised eyebrows of curved cornices.

Round the tip, then, but out far enough to see the Lady of Liberty hold her torch and feel the strong damp Atlantic wind and hear gulls screaming and pass a freighter outward bound under a grove of derricks. And look with distaste at the abandoned buildings on Ellis Island where so many frightened, ignorant foreigners first met America, helpless in the bureaucracy of freedom.

Then turning east and north and pointing into the East River and under that still most beautiful of its spans, the Brooklyn Bridge, the wired web of delicacy, that cat's cradle of tension, inconceivably supporting a great weight of traffic. And under, gliding oceanward, comes the long gray guided-missile cruiser *Topeka,* her full complement of men lining her decks, face outward at attention, her small orange darts pointing skyward aft, and her radar intricacies listening for sonic images. There she was, translating in steel the desperate speeches of Pentagon admirals committed to a navy without a future:

The New York I Know

80

beautiful, armed, and obsolete.

The East River is a strange river because it has such an ugly beauty. Ugly, that is, in its lack of verge or greenery except on Welfare Island and the leafy lawn of Sutton Place. The waterfronts of industrial cities all share the shabby clutter of business, but abroad a river bank is an excuse for beauty too, a place where the city man can rest and breathe, bending his gaze on the strong or placid current. On the East River these pleasures are reserved mostly for apartment dwellers, at a remove of many paces and feet. The only people who can get close enough for intimacy must choose between a rotting pier or a few parks separated from the actual bank by the East Side Highway, a rival and distracting current of cars. Only from the UN, the Lower Sixties, and Carl Schurz Park is there no such interposition.

Yet the East River is made romantic by its shipping, which ranges from barges and excursion boats to ponderous tankers and polished yachts, by its procession of bridges, and by its magnificent Manhattan shore, far different from the profile turned to the Hudson. For it is a shore of extremes in living, making the eye jump its entire length from the doomed tenements of the lower East Side to the serene thin slab of the Secretariat, a marble mirror for light; from grimy coal chutes and power stations to the new white serrated luxury apartment buildings at Beekman and Sutton Places and at Gracie Square. All these disparate elements—even the factory chimneys, even the Pepsi-Cola sign on the Brooklyn shore—contribute to a mysterious and

The
Waterways

81

exciting whole, the natural rhythm of a useful river. Only one element obtrudes and spoils: the public housing units. These are grim cities within themselves, cities—since the living are invisible—of the dead. Utility and economy need not be companions of ugliness, but here they are. These are premature tombs in which the human spirit is confined in a rigid and graceless coffin of convenience, identically ventilated by identical windows with its legion of neighbors, refused the small benedictions of decoration or difference. One argues that this is better than decaying slums, that people have light and air and plumbing and the sweep of the river, that children have space for play. But there is still something not only wrong but sinister in these arbitrary groupings of human life, and the wiser city planners are troubled by it. To the river traveler, certainly, they are depressants, casting a chill on the mind.

In my childhood, the chill was cast by Welfare Island, or Blackwell's as it was called then, that quarantine of the ill and insane between two tines of water. The original hospitals can still be seen behind the lawns and trees: Gothic and dark and sad, hiding (those years ago) unmentionable things and incurable troubles. A few are still used, but most are deserted, and one —with breached walls and shattered windows—is a training ground for rookie firemen, the object of required abuse. New buildings are on the island now, light and modern; and although they too house suffering, they cast no similar shadow as you pass by. Pity is subtituted for horror, and also relief that society has abandoned

82

83

the architecture of despair. Only the new big yellow buildings for the insane on Ward's Island have an institutional cruelty, but at least they are light and spacious, though thickly barred.

Unlike the Hudson, it is the little intimacies that make the East River absorbing: the tiny huddle of Georgian brick houses on Sutton Place with their common garden, overwhelmed by surrounding apartment heights; the little girls playing basketball on the roof of the Brearley School over a tunnel of traffic; the squat anachronism of what used to be a serene and lordly landmark on the river shore, Gracie Mansion; the signs on pilings, "Swimmers Keep Off," in the heat of summer, unread and unheeded as thin boys plunge in the dirty current. And as the East River turns westward and narrows into the Harlem River, these intimacies multiply to the total exclusion of grandeur. The shores of the Harlem River are messy fringes, the neglected back yards of the poor. Only at the tip of Harlem at "Sugar Hill" do the apartments of the well-to-do Negroes display ordered living; and on the Bronx side, much further back, a residential ridge of propriety. The rest is broken piers, mud flats, and old boathouses, sagging into the river; mountainous heaps of junked cars, a pattern of twisted fenders; a disused railroad bridge with the center span swung—and fixed forever—in midstream.

But then, gradually, the banks of the Harlem River prepare themselves for the future: rocks appear, and cliffs, and trees, and the eye turns upwards to the playing grounds of Columbia, to Baker Field,

The New York I Know

84

to parkland and more rocks and cliffs. Then down to the river again and stalwart young men on the dock of the university boathouse, and further on to other young men in sculls, resting on their oars, their crew cuts catching the sun, their legs at ease. The hint of freedom is there even before the iron railroad bridge at the mouth of the Harlem opens to let you by. And then, with a rush of wind and a great expansion of focus, the Hudson River rides past. Two miles ahead to the West the Palisades rear up, a wall of vertical stone folds with a crest of woods. To the north, the winding, converging, rolling shores suggest the far-hidden mountain source in the heart of the state. To the south, the widening water hurries to its assignation with greater water. And once you have flowed with it under the splendor of the George Washington span, the meaning of rivers rushes over you. So too does the feel of an earlier America with broader, more venturesome men, the feel of original wildness and hazard, and the feel of conquest. Rather than shrink in comparison, the nature of man reassumes its stature.

As for the city itself, south of this bridge, it is a clean and fairly unbroken line of highway and park and residence, built high. Riverside Drive has long given the Hudson its due as a great prospect for dwellers, and here Manhattan assumes a consistent if unexciting face: a hundred and thirty blocks or about eight miles of apartment buildings facing it and the setting sun behind Jersey; the homes of the middle class who pay for their privilege with the biting gales of winter, a certain inconvenience of

The New York
I Know

transit, and the knowledge that their address confers no social benefits. They know too that behind them are blighted streets and dubious neighborhoods, but the river is compensation and daily solace.

Yet, after all, and when the river voyage is done, the sight from the Upper Bay still remains the dream, and a self-perpetuating one at that. It is no less valid now than it was thirty journeys ago, to a child coming home from summer abroad at the prow of a ship.

There were differences then: the decks below me were filled with steerage passengers, a huddle of immigrants in kerchiefs, holding bundles. They smelled, they were ragged, they had been seasick most of the way, they were cold, they were afraid. To a child without compassion, they were as repellent as they were pitiable. I did not want to be near them. But at this moment as the ship approached New York, even I saw the look in their eyes as they saw the Statue of Liberty and the first stand of towers. The children were transfixed. The parents wept, some aloud, some wiping their tears away with stiffened hands, some letting them run down. Even the youths were quiet. I had read about the promised land, I had been told what immigrants were, I knew that my grandparents had pulled their lives out of Europe too for this same dream. Now I knew what it meant.

And somehow, the things I have learned since then make no difference now. Bartholdi's statue is not great art, not even impressive art, but the Lady is invested with greatness by each new eye. The vision of New York as the promised land can be turned into a sour joke, so cruel can the city be, so qualified its welcome. From this distance corruption cannot be smelt, nor decay, nor venality. The bungling and stuttering of little men in capitals of state or nation cannot be perceived from the Upper Bay, nor the sound of broken illusions.

This is the port of America, these are the heralding towers of the New World.

The New York I Know

88

5. *Broadway*

ALTHOUGH BROADWAY'S only reason for being is the theater, the name covers more than a single artery and less than the capital of entertainment in the United States. More, because Broadway includes the side streets east to Sixth Avenue and west to Eighth Avenue; less, because although all the major theaters are housed in this area, they are only a part of the life that breathes its air. Here the extremes of innocence and corruption meet, and the mecca for performers and their public is also an open ward—unstaffed, unsupervised, unlocked—for people without purpose or with low purpose.

The real innocence of Broadway is seldom visible to a visitor. It resides on the stage of an empty, darkened theater, where six or ten or fifty people in casual dress sit or move or talk under the tired light of a bare bulb and heed the voices of dark shapes in the empty orchestra. In the days of rehearsal, when a play is born, hope and excitement fill the cavernous air. To these men and women and boys and girls, to the actor, the dancer, the singer, the director, the jazz musician, this illusion is the passionate reality, the whole of life. What is outside it or beyond it is a distant dream, and the only purity, call it dedication, that you will find in Broadway is in this wall-less realm. For performance is an act of faith. When a boy dances or a girl sings or an actor speaks his lines, he believes not only in what he is but what he does in the moment of doing it. Whether he is alone in a cold theater or warmed by an audience, this belief is his utter immunity. If the play or musical keeps running, each performance is a renewal of faith, and the magic contact between player and public a pure joy. If the play closes, the tragedy for the performer and writer is also pure, and grief another immunity. Only these conditions of being protect them from the terrible commerce of Broadway theater as it now exists, which can no longer afford to recognize that area between success and failure where truth so often lives.

For on Broadway money rules. Like a host of vultures, the ticket brokers, the speculators, the craft unions, the agents, the backers, the real estate owners move in on the creative body and take their bite. The world of dreams breathes in an iron lung; and without this mechanical pumping it dies.

You see this greed in a Broadway first-night audience, of all manifestations one of the least innocent. For these people come not to give but to take, not to see but to be shown. They come to judge as buyers judge: Is the stuff worth my money or isn't it? Although some still dress for the occasion, there is nothing festive in their attendance and nothing gentle in their attitudes. "They," admittedly, are not all first-nighters: there are always the nervous and hopeful friends and those, stage-struck and audience-struck, for whom presence at a first performance is an addiction.

Nevertheless, the Broadway audience at any per-

The New York I Know

92

formance of any hit is a very different public from the playgoers of twenty years ago. The stamp of vulgarity is there, of indulgence, or coarse fiber. What is conspicuously no longer there is courtesy, whether toward fellow spectators or the performers. And a Broadway charity audience turns the theater into a convention hall, with recognition and gossip taking precedence over the play.

Everything, in fact, in this theater capital takes precedence over talent, without which it could not exist, and over brave new thinking, without which it may sink even further into the cutthroat business it has become.

The innocence is confined to the stage itself and those who perform there. But on the streets of Broadway are other innocents: the tourist transients who believe that Broadway is exciting, or rather who feel that it must be. You can spot them easily, for the difference between the out-of-towner and the native is marked by approach as much as by attire. Walking slowly, they gaze at the "sights" without expression: up at the huge electric signs and sideways at the half-naked women on movie marquees. They drag their listless children behind them; the women with fussy little white hats and too many colors and accessories, the men—in open-neck sport shirts or two-toned cardigans— dressed for the barbecue pit. Up and down they walk on Broadway, where nothing in this entertainment world seems to divert or delight them but where the fact of having been there will be their reward.

*The New York
I Know*

94

You can see them eating in a fishbowl restaurant, pale in the neon light as they chew their jumbo burgers; you can see them lingering outside a record shop as rock n' roll blasts at them from within; but these days you hardly ever see them going into a movie house or a theater. It is not shows they want, but sights; and they are not at all sure what sights they expect to see or want to see. They have been on Broadway.

The other innocents are the soldiers and sailors, for they come there for a high time, ready to spend their accumulated pay for everything from a steak dinner to a strip tease, from a real chick to a movie about lost girls in nudist camps. Slowly they amble up Broadway, their eyes cruising and catching the eyes of girls who are looking for them. On every block these girls saunter, some not more than fifteen years old, their buttocks hard in toreador pants, their eyes like houris', their mouths exercised on gum and obscenity. There is nothing they have not known since they were six except love, and nothing they are prepared to give for nothing. If the signals work, the boys and the girls will join at a bar on Eighth Avenue. And the next day the boys will boast of Broadway and broads while their heads are heavy as stones, their mouths full of ashes and their wallets empty. And those who found no girls will make them up.

To the innocents, the true hideousness of Broadway is neither apparent nor disturbing. The urban American, no matter where he lives, except perhaps in San Francisco or Washington, D.C., is so condi-

The New York I Know

96

tioned to ugliness that the squalor of Broadway at daytime and the twitching glitter of Broadway at night are only matters of degree compared to his downtown Main Street. There is more of everything, including people; and quantity has for so long been sold us as a substitute for quality that it exerts a fascination for those who have never known the nature of worth.

It is on this ignorance that the predators feed, giving much of Broadway the shabby tawdriness of a boardwalk in a cheap resort. Here Harry the Hick can buy a rubber belly dancer or a denture ashtray; and Lou-Ann can buy Fabian beanies for her kids. The merchandise is uniformly hideous, but it must sell, for the merchants stay in business year after year, relying on fresh waves of innocence and provincialism from other cities.

The honky-tonk of Broadway has its special odors too: peanuts roasting, pizzas and burgers and frankfurters frying in old grease, and the chocolate breath of candy shops. There is a certain smell from the cheap luggage stores, too, not so much leather as plastic, and one of musty paper from the jumbles of secondhand books. Then there is the strong chicken smell of broilers barbecuing in rows on spits, and the strong beef-and-charcoal smell from the steakhouses, where the red-faced old promoters and press agents and politicians eat, and the charge-account boys from the Middle West and the West.

Broadway But is there not in all this, you might say, a surging vitality, a sense of bustle and health? Broadway

97

is the home of jazz and comics and performing frenzy and the quick buck: it has a fast pulse and a glittering eye. In the blaring lights, windows of clarinets, trombones, bongo drums, and saxophones wheel and overlap with the nudes, the marquees, and the endless parade of feet like an old-fashioned montage set to rapid blues. But this is surface excitement only, enticing the bored, the bewildered, or the profoundly naïve. Its essence is akin to the St. Vitus's dance of the young punks around juke boxes: a mindless jerking devoid of joy or gaiety.

Even the raw sex of the striptease joints is deadly serious, for the customers if not for the providers. The hush in the dark as the women approximate copulation in the light is so dense that the men appear not to breathe at all; their total stillness a cover for their inward stirring, their assumption of clinical study fooling none.

Broadway never sleeps, but Broadway is full of places for sleeping. Every so often in the obituary pages of the New York papers a paragraph like this appears: "Mary Belle Blossom, Actress" . . . "Miss Blossom, known as Broadway Belle in the early twenties, died at the age of seventy-five, after a long illness. Although noted for her musical comedy roles in such hits as 'Kiss Me, Willy,' and 'Oh, You Kid,' Miss Blossom is also remembered for character parts in such road company productions as 'Mother's Angel' and 'What Katy Did.' She was found dead in her room at the King George Hotel, where she had resided for the last

The New York I Know

thirty years. Miss Blossom leaves no survivors."

The entrances of the King Georges are barely discernible between the bar signs and pizza counters and music shops that crowd them on either side; the air in their grimy lobbies and halls is stale from want of oxygen and soap and water, and the passage of a thousand nights of smokers; their windows are never washed, and on the sills higher up you will see in winter the cartons of milk and the paper bags of fruit which people like Mary Belle have no other place to cool. There can be no peace, ever, in these rooms because the neon circuits never fail, and those lit by their flashings all night long must either be nerveless, drunk, or drugged, or themselves work at night and sleep by day.

Who are they? Some transients of course, bedding as cheaply as they can nearest to the distractions they want, but mostly people whose jobs or hopes bind them to these streets: jazz musicians, bit actors, nightclub waiters, old promoters, young fixers, whores, and all the fringe that cling like drowning fingers on the edge of the raft of show-business. Those on the raft do not live in the King Georges: they do not have to. Nor, indeed, do the residents have to, except through a kind of sickness, a profound delusion of self that leads them to believe that here is life and they are at its center.

There are better hotels in the Broadway district; a few old ones that manage somehow to retain a certain decency and propriety, hospitable mainly to working professionals or old ladies of good habits; and the newly remodeled big brash ones, where the sightseers and the business people go. These are harshly modern and brilliantly lit and they might be anywhere across the country. They have the chain stamp: the same coffee, the same paper mats, the same service without solicitude that has made our hotels the automated and charmless shelters they are.

In any case, the transients in these big places are mostly outsiders coming to find excitement, glamour, or profit on Broadway; and the regular patrons of the little shabby places are the insiders, for whom it is life.

Between them are the street dwellers, who live nowhere: those without purpose, destination, or address. And a walk on Forty-second Street from Broadway to Eighth Avenue will show you all you want of the dislocated. These are the youths who mill around to fill their emptiness with feelings of violence in a dozen different ways: by the shabby sex movies that promise Savage Rites and Naked Abandon in blowups showing the straining breasts of bound women; in "bookstores" that offer a mountainous clutter of pornography along with the current paperbacks; in windows of knives where a thicket of blades stab and glitter; in record stores where in a blaze of lights a blare of sound pounds on the ears and the thumping beat of idiot lyrics drowns out thought; in fun parlors where they can shoot or play Fascination for hours, filling nothingness with the click of balls. All these are oxygen for stillborn souls.

Broadway   What these boys cannot stand is silence. And it is

103

hard to tell whether the juke-box beat they twitch to soothes their savage breasts or, again, merely provides one more insulation from an unbearable reality. They share with the older drifters—the red-eyed unshaven alcoholics who weave and shuffle—a world without shape.

No, Broadway takes shape only on its stages, and nowhere else. Unlike Forty-second Street or the cross streets in the Forties east of Fifth Avenue, the streets west of it, between Broadway and Eighth, are dedicated to the business of the theater, with only a few bars and restaurants to distract from the playhouse façades, marquees, and entrances. Soberly dark after midnight, discreet and closed in the mornings and five afternoons in the week, they burst into light and bustle at night and on matinee days, opening up to a tide of people and disgorging them two hours later.

On a street like Forty-fifth with six theaters along one block, eight-thirty is the hour of acceleration and expectation as the cabs stream up and the play-goers swarm and policemen on horseback direct the converging currents. Then the myth of Broadway becomes fact, and the word "smash hit" are electric in meanings as well as in signs. Then there is destination in these streets, and a natural purpose.

And after the theater, a place like Sardi's has its purpose too, or rather a double purpose: to key up the spectators while it unwinds the performers. What it sells, beyond food, is the sense of status that the presence of celebrities seems to confer on some; and, to the celebrities themselves, a place for

shop talk among their peers, a place to be seen without effort, a tangible measure of their success. It is, above all, the tavern of the profession, open to the unprofessional. And although it is an obvious target of satire—the hopeful starlet pretending poise but alert to all glances, the TV "personalities" saluting right and left, the press agents plying their trade from table to table, the flutter of "darlings" from the lips while the eyes appraise—vitality is there too, and that special warmth which actors always bestow as the charming, decorative, eternal innocents they are.

Was Broadway always like this? In certain ways, yes. the tourists, the drifters, the bums, the petty crooks, the young on the prowl, the barflies, the purveyors of vice—these have always belonged to it. The lights have always dazzled at night and the blaze of theater marquees (more golden in my youth in the absence of neon) has always gathered the playgoing moths in clusters.

What then is the difference of years? Two things, mostly. One is the astounding emptiness of most of the big movie-house lobbies. The braided footmen are there, the woman sits in the glass box office, but except for a smash hit like *Ben-Hur* there are not only no lines of people as there used to be, but hours with no one at all buying a ticket. And this for pictures performed by stars and well reviewed.

Television has killed the newsreel houses as it has killed vaudeville, having pre-empted both functions; and there are few places now where a half hour could be spent between appointments to be informed or amused.

Broadway always had the gaudy cheapness of any center of popular entertainment, but there seems little question that physical deterioration and an increase in shoddiness and vulgarity have in the last two decades gone hand in hand, to the detriment of the city and its citizens. Parts of Broadway are blighted areas, the perfect setting not only for sporadic sins but for vice organized on a big and dangerous scale. Good people live everywhere, and Broadway has its share: the cheerful waitresses, the brave old failures, the genial drunks, the generous delicatessen owners, the yearning and vulnerable young with dreams of glory. But they live in a citadel of cynicism, where the human being is a sucker since he was born, and where there is no place between fame and failure where he can live and work. This is the major brutality Broadway imposes on its one reason for being: the theater.

Broadway

107

108

6. *City Voices*

Taxis:

Sixty-fifth, going east to Lexington: "Look at those cars double-parked. Ever see 'em get a ticket? Not them. Ain't a cop don't get his payoff for letting 'em park."

Broadway and Fiftieth, going south: "They're all crooks, from the Mayor down. You tell me, you tell me one thing this Mayor's done for this city! One thing! They're all lousy politicians."

Seventy-fifth Street, going west to Park Avenue: "Boy I could tell this Mayor how to clean up this mess. If he had any guts, he could do it. Now, if we had La Guardia . . . ."

To Idlewild: "So my son, he says, Pop you got to get rid of all that furniture, I'm gonna buy you modern, see he gets two thousand a month in that electronics business he works for, he likes to spend, but I say, look, your mother and I we bought that when we got married and it's good enough, and after she died, you know, it sort of keeps me company, I'm used to it. But these young people they always want new things, new things, even if they're made cheap, but what can I do, my kid's smart, he knows what he wants . . . ."

South on Seventh: "Oh boy, did I have a night—no, not drinking, just arguing with my wife. She al-

109

ways wants this, she wants that, she's got status on her mind, she says, Mannie, this coat ain't what they're wearing now, and I say what the hell's the matter with it, it looks okay, and she says I go out in this and I feel like a dog, this year it's wrap-around or whatever. Same thing with furniture, now she wants a hot-tray, what do we need with a hot-tray, she don't cook, we always eat out . . . ."

Gramercy Park, going east: "So what, the Chinese are commies, they're there, ain't they, they run the place . . . so what are we doing with Chiang Kai-shek, he's just a small-time dictator? I don't get this Formosa bit . . . ."

Remodeled brownstone, two flights up, white room hung with abstractions:

" . . . calligraphy."

"Yes, it's pushing outside its limits . . . ."

"What do you expect from the *Times?* They're just catching up with Wyeth . . . ."

"Mies once said . . . ."

"You feel the tension in this space. It pulls the vertical downward."

"Well, I thought $5,000 was big, but Kurt said it's a big picture, people are buying them big . . . ."

Hardware store, proprietor to customer; January: "Well, I sent the wife and kids down to the Fountainblue, I'm going next week. Yeah, forty a day, but they're all like that, and anyhow you need a break in winter . . . ."

Delicatessen owner to friend: "Well I told Char-

The New York I Know

110

lene—she's only sixteen, you know—I said, no, baby, I will not give you ten dollars to dye your hair, why do you want to dye your hair? and you shoulda heard the squawk that kid put up, crying and all, so her mother says oh let her do it, Irv, they're all doing it, so what's the harm, and I say at *her* age for Christ's sake, but you know women, they never let go . . . ."

Liquor store dealer to customer: "Sorry, I got no one to deliver, two of my boys didn't come in because of the rain. Honest, lady, it's terrible these days, nobody wants to work, they just stay away when they feel like it, so what, they get paid anyhow or they get another job. Nobody cares, I tell you, nobody cares."

Shoe store manager to customer: "Yes, you're right, they didn't match the sample. What can you do? They don't care, you see, they got no pride in their work, it's the same all over. The union protects 'em no matter what they do, why should they care?"

Passenger to bus driver: "But you always used to make this stop . . . . "

Bus driver to passenger: "Well we ain't now, so move on back, you're blocking the passage . . . . "

Apartment living room in the East Seventies, after dinner; the women, segregated: "Thank you, darling—it's only junk, but I loved the design."

"If they can clean they can't cook and vice versa. Marie is really a divine cook but quite crazy. She came in just before a large dinner the other night

*The New York
I Know*

and said, Madame, he is there with a big knife again!"

"You have to use sour cream. It's no good without it . . . . "

"Do you really think I am? Well, I'm sticking to Metrecal for lunch, mostly."

The men, segregated: "I told Nelson I didn't think he could swing it, but . . . . "

"They're asking six thousand an acre now, so as an investment it can't . . . . "

"Hong Kong. They only cost ten bucks, made to order . . . . "

"I still maintain the economy can't take it. You pour nine billion into . . . . "

Women, anywhere in the city:

"Well, I'm not all that crazy about mink; there's too much of it around anyway . . . . "

"It was a doll of a dress, you know, kinda tight around here and loose here, with a darling collar . . . . "

"I always go to her, she knows my taste, the other day . . . . "

". . . so Mannie comes in and says what the hell you do to your hair, and I said for God's sake Mannie sometimes you get tired of your face . . . . "

"Well I told her, don't let him get away with it, he knows perfectly well what he's doing, why should she put up with it? she's got money of her own anyway . . . . "

The New York
I Know

114

Men, anywhere in the city:

"So I said, fifty thousand? What do you take me for?"

"As I get it, the deal is, a million down and . . . . "

"So if you sell for five, the least you ought to count on is . . . . "

"With that margin, I don't see how you can lose, especially if the amortization . . . . "

"So I said no dough, that job's worth two hundred a week or I . . . . "

"Sure you can take it off your tax, Ed told me . . . . "

I have eavesdropped in many cities: Rome, Paris, Berlin, Madrid; but nowhere have I heard more constant talk of money at all levels and in all places than in New York. And I do not mean talk in places and hours of business. I mean talk in good restaurants over lunch or dinner, talk in living rooms and theaters, talk in buses and on street corners, talk at cocktail parties, automats, and lunch counters. It is talk of money that animates the men, of deals, tips, investments, pay checks, overtime, and all the ways in which a dollar can be doubled. I eavesdrop in vain for the kind of talk I hear on the streets of Europe: French cabdrivers arguing about politics, men in British pubs fighting about the Labour Party, Italian masons fulminating about German tourists; talk of food and women, talk—on earth and street level—of ideas. All people talk of money sometimes, everywhere. But not for all people, everywhere, is money the addiction, the obsession, the

City Voices

stimulant, that it seems to be in New York. It is a
large part of the clamor, and it is the voice—quite
literally—of the man in the street.

Within the tall walls of New York are tens of
thousands of voices talking of other things: of
books and medicine, of plays and acting, of scholars
and policy, of faith and death. Again, the glory of
New York is this diversity, in which any man can
match his own speech, whether in the vocabulary of
psychiatry or art or religion or sport, or in the alien
tongues and accents that make this city more than
American. Walk on West Side streets or in the park
and you will hear the heavy consonants and rounded
vowels of the Austrian and German Jews who fled
to the city in the thirties, or the high sibilant Spanish chatter of the Puerto Ricans—two sounds that
have replaced the Irish brogue and the Italian reci-
tative in much of New York. Babel it still is, though
the idioms change.

But what, in his way of talking, marks the long-
term or native New Yorker apart from most other
Americans, who in turn recognize his difference? It
is not merely a matter of Bronx or Brooklyn accents, unique to this city. It is a matter, very hard to
define, of intonation and phrasing that produces a
sophistication absent in the voices of the Midwest,
the Far West, and the South. Unlike them, New
York is a region only in attitude. The New York
voice reflects its diversity, its foreignness, and, inev-
itably, the sense of superiority New Yorkers feel or
come to feel. It says, without saying, We Know.
And nowhere is this assumption of vantage more

*The New York
I Know*

116

clearly evident than in the casual drawl of the upper-class, traveled man or woman, who throws words away as mink coats are tossed on chairs. To the Midwesterner, on the other hand, words are serious, and each syllable is given the same attention.

In the poorer purlieus, southern Negro and Puerto Rican influence has served to thicken and blur the New York speech so that much of what the young New Yorker of the streets has to say is impenetrable; only the spit of contempt comes through. I do not for a moment suppose this city is alone in the debasement of language by poor diction and almost total reliance on obscenity, but the street children of New York—of whatever origin and color—bring the Word to its knees. They do not speak; they rape.

Yet beautiful speech is here too, in abundance; where actors gather, where teachers explain, where singers practice their songs, and where young students from the far corners of the world translate their thoughts into English with awkward purity. The voice of New York is scored for a great orchestra, even if some of the instruments are stridently harsh. And if the chorus does not sing "Seid umschlungen, millionen!" the theme of the symphony is still freedom. Each voice, to those who listen, can be heard.

City Voices

119

7. *Vie de Bohème*

I DON'T KNOW JUST HOW I discovered Greenwich Village somewhere in the twenties, but I suspect I posed for an artist who lived there. I had the sort of face that enthralled painters and discouraged boys, and I know that from fifteen on I spent much of my time standing, sitting, and lying in studios draped in loose garments while men paced back and forth, squinted, laid on pigment or pushed clay, and talked of bone structure, themselves, and me. And since most of them worked and lived in the Village, I began to know the streets and the life and the studios quite well.

Not only did Greenwich Village have the savor of the Europe I loved from early childhood; it stood for a kind of rebellion against the life of musicians I was beginning to find too respectable. I knew my parents were artists, but they were very moral too; and the atmosphere of hard work, regular meals, and *gemütlichkeit* was beginning to bear rather heavily on a girl steeped in bad, as well as good, romantic literature and determined, at whatever cost, to live dangerously. A studio was obviously the place to do it in, and I already saw myself as a modern Maja Desnuda or Madame X on the walls of the Metropolitan, driving men mad with desire.

It was with some surprise, therefore, and suppressed chagrin that I found the studio little more sinful than the music room, and the artist—by and large—just as serious. What happened in the north lights and whitewashed walls of Greenwich Village houses was not the toppling of virtue so much as the expansion of vision: I began to see things I had never seen before; not only objects but a way of looking at them, not only shapes but a way of feeling them. My ears had been opened to sound since birth, and the structure of music had entered my being. But although my parents had innate good taste and my mother could have been an accomplished landscape painter—her sketches had great sensibility and form—musicians are less aware, I think, than all other creative people of the specific pleasures of the eye. The homes of most of the virtuosi and conductors and singers and composers I knew in youth were densely cluttered, curtained and tasseled, and suffused with the green of potted ferns. I could never understand how they could manage to divorce the beauty of sound from the beauty of sight, but they did. They were quite happy in their airless nests.

The bareness of the studio, then, came as a revelation. In this white purity, lit evenly and coldly by skylights, every object in the room had meaning. In Greenwich Village I first saw animal skulls, bleached; empty bottles chosen for their shape; artifacts from Mexico or New Mexico; fruit in huge bowls; woven cloths of strong colors from exotic places; plain wood tables, unvarnished; windows

*The New York
I Know*

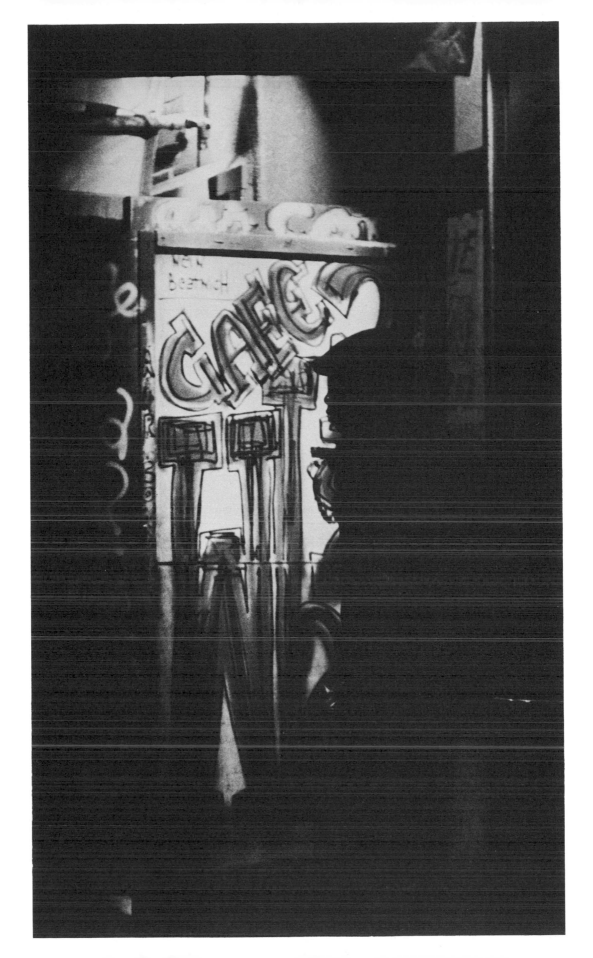

without curtains; pillows on floors; and studio couches.

In Greenwich Village I first saw Artists' Wives. I seem to remember that they all wore bangs, were inclined to fleshiness, and were all dressed in full skirts and peasant blouses when the fashion was knee-length sheaths. Instead of single long strands of pearls, they wore hammered silver and turquoise matrix. Even more remarkable, they could all cook fragrant spaghetti and exotic stews. Uptown, German or Irish or Finnish cooks made the solid meals, heavy with potatoes and dumplings.

In Greenwich Village I first heard people speak of breasts and thighs and buttocks and bellies as one would speak of mountains and rivers and bread and fruit; and I first discovered that it was possible to look at a naked body impersonally as form and texture and substance.

In Greenwich Village I first heard sex talked of with joy and amusement as an open delight and not a secret urge. And if all these revelations sound unimaginably naïve to a generation drilled in four-letter words and the techniques of intercourse, I can only say that people like my parents were not only inhibited but fastidious, and found much ugly that we now find routine. In consequence, my pose as *femme fatale,* heavily borrowed from the bookshelves, concealed a staggering innocence. Greenwich Village, in the animal simplicity that resides in most painters, played a large part in dissipating it, without shock or squalor.

What is more, Washington Square and the streets

The New York
I Know

124

of the Village themselves presented a kind of city living entirely different from the Upper West Side, and all the more alluring because of it. The avenues where I grew up—Amsterdam, Broadway, Columbus—were, as I have written, unrelievedly ugly, and although the brownstone rows of the side streets then spelled peace and security, they were still no treat to the eye. Only the Hudson River brought beauty, but too grand and remote a beauty to live with in daily intimacy. In the Village, the red brick houses surrounding the leafy, green, and sunlit Square gave me (as the one remaining northern row still gives) a welling of pleasure, and to walk down Tenth or Eleventh Street, west of Fifth, was—and is—to know the gay serenity of light and sky above low buildings designed—with their broad windows and wide fronts—for the important human needs of space, proportion, comfort, and dignity. Inside, the fires burned in the marble fireplaces, books reached to the ceiling, and prints from Piranesi to Picasso hung, at spare intervals, on the high walls.

These, of course, were the finer homes of the Village, lived in by producers, the more successful writers, a few "old families," and the dilettantes who breathe freest in the atmosphere of the arts and form their essential audience. Most of the painters and sculptors and artisans lived either on the Square (if they sold enough) or in the little houses in the crooked streets around Sheridan Square and west of Seventh.

Then as now, poor or rich, successes or failures, *The New York I Know*

126

the Villagers could stroll in the streets, sit in the cafés, buy an abundance of fresh produce and foreign staples very cheaply, eat in good restaurants, and drink good wine as a matter of course. They could also live together without being married, without shame, and with impunity. This, I thought, was civilized living. And my visits to the Village, first in innocence and later in involvement, constituted not only a release from convention, which is negative, but a new, and positive, experience of freedom.

For years now, the Village has constituted neither for me: few of my friends now live there, and freedom has long since become an interior matter. But as an outsider, who visits from curiosity only, that part of New York still performs its function as a sanctuary from the savage pressures of the surrounding city, a close-knit community proud of its physical difference and its human diversity, clinging tenaciously to its narrowing ground. In spite of the encroachment of new buildings and new elements, the composition of the Village has changed very little from earlier times. The Italians, who formed its oldest community, are still there, speaking Italian. A new generation of working artists and writers lives there, producing. Dilettantes still abound, and so do people with humdrum jobs who prefer the Village way of life and can afford the rents now asked for well-kept apartments. Young professionals still raise good families there while *Vie* they fight for liberal causes and better government. *de Bohème* And although the Square itself has suffered heavily

127

from the steady growth of New York University and the cheaply modern apartment house at its southeast corner, much of the Village has remained visually the same: low little houses, intimate handiwork shops, a profusion of foodstalls, and the amiable clutter that small businesses and impractical methods usually produce.

Even the tourists have not changed much, for the Village was always a show. Camera-hung, curious, ordinary, innocent, they come from all the states to see how Artists live, to buy souvenirs, to sample Vice, to take pictures of quaint corners, and stare at beatniks. There they stroll, pointing at little shop-windows full of crude leather sandals or Danish pottery or abstract silver jewelry, or those bright bisexual pants and sweaters; peering down at dirty basement doors scrawled with cabalistic letters promising far-out entertainment at night; sitting uneasily in the dim espresso bars, seeing the people I saw. Were these the White Negroes Norman Mailer wrote about?

It is on this bleak scene that a phenomenon has appeared: the American existentialist—the hipster, the man who knows that if our collective condition is to live with instant death by atomic war, . . . or with a slow death by comformity with every creative and rebellious instinct stifled (at what damage to the mind and the heart and the liver and the nerves no research foundation for cancer will discover in a hurry), if the fate of twentieth-century man is to live with death from adolescence to premature senescence, why then the only life-giving answer is to accept the terms of death, to

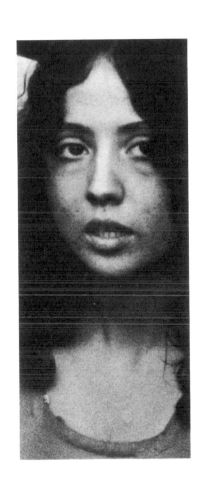

live with death as immediate danger, to divorce oneself from society, to exist without roots, to set out on that uncharted journey into the rebellious imperatives of the self. In short, whether the life is criminal or not, the decision is to encourage the psychopath in oneself, to explore that domain of experience where security is boredom and therefore sickness, and one exists in the present, in that enormous present which is without past or future, memory or planned intention, the life where a man must go until he is beat, where he must gamble with his energies through all those small or large crises of courage and unforeseen situations which beset his day, where he must be with it or doomed not to swing.

The girls with white faces of death and streaming hair, the unshaven or bearded boys in heavy turtle necks (like the girls'): were these the psychopaths Robert Lindner described who, like children, like hipsters, "cannot delay the pleasures of gratification . . . [which] explains not only [their] behaviour but also the violent nature of [their] acts"? There was indeed a childishness about these unclean young people acting out their charades of rebellion and defiance, pretending dark knowledge and invulnerability, moving from kick to trance. Most of them, I am told, do not live in the Village: they come from ordinary homes in the Bronx or Brooklyn or the Upper West Side, spending their days and some of their nights in this different, tolerant air, far from the deadening talk of money and work in their parents' parlors. Some are schoolboys and girls, boarding a subway to the Village after classes in search of pornography or perver-

sion. Some are N.Y.U. students using it as a campus, the Village a convenient annex for the pursuit of special studies or the practice of loafing.

Like the tourists, I stared at the commuting Negroes sitting with white girls, the commuting Negro women sitting with white men, their faces sleepily arrogant, saying in effect: Take a good look—that's the way it is. They too were acting: a performance of rights taken and equality claimed in the brotherhood of Hip. Wherever they moved, the implication of violence moved with them, like a cloud. The Village was where they need not wait for gratification; indeed, they forced it. I saw too, in the white girl partners, the superiority of a hunter who has bagged rare game. The pose of the Negro was boredom; the boast would wait for Harlem.

As for the commuting homosexuals, white and Negro, their languid postures and lazy obscenities are, even more, challenges flung in the public face. As in the heterosexual pairing of race, they are not merely living as they choose to live and cannot elsewhere. They are thrusting themselves on society, consciously committing acts of aggression on observers who betray their aversion.

It is, indeed, this joyless self-consciousness and this threat of violence that makes the Greenwich Village I now see as a tourist a different place from the Greenwich Village I knew before. There is nothing new and nothing wrong in the rebellious and restless young seeking a refuge for their differences: we too sat around in cafés and speakeasies strangely

The New York
I Know

132

attired and carelessly groomed, making our own world. We too proclaimed our right to promiscuity and experiment, confessing proudly to dark urges. We too preferred the warmth and intimacy of Village streets to the barren respectability of the uptown reaches. We too found color and excitement in the company of artists and actors, artisans and playwrights, sculptors and poets. Some of our best friends were failures.

As for squares, we felt the same contempt for Babbitts. We even had our beatniks, with this difference: ours worked, or talked of working. And here again is another gap between today's rebels and us: we not only believed that a better world was possible but that we could make it. The pose of nihilism requires passivity; the act of nihilism implies destruction. The Village beats, commuting and resident, either do nothing or do harm. Where we may have committed violence against ourselves, through drink or despair, they commit violence against the image of man by assuming that their chaos is his truth.

I am speaking mainly of the show-offs, the exhibits, the Village extras that clip-joints prey on and a visitor sees. And if I linger on them, it is because they—and those who make money from them—have almost pushed the stars off the stage and taken over the play.

Greenwich Village was the natural home of the artist in New York; the only place where rents were low, the light unblocked by high buildings, unrefracted by reflecting walls of glass. Here artists

Vie
de Bohème

133

could live cheaply and simply, meeting each other without planning, behaving freely without the inhibitions and attention of a formal society. Here, in this quiet backwater, they could escape the competitive frenzy of commercial uptown and financial downtown and allow the small pleasures to flower.

Many artists still live there for those reasons, though the reasons are daily diluted. The rents for good studios are now so high that artists cannot afford them: only the well-to-do who like big rooms and the aura, if not the substance, of art. Most of the working painters now live in rows of near-tenements or loft buildings on the streets near Third and Second Avenues, from Eighth to Fourteenth. They have their light and their enclosed company; they are even a "school" of painting, but they do not share those specific visual and community charms long clustered around the nuclei of Washington and Sheridan Squares. Possibly, since their eyes are turned inward, they do not need them: it is their fortune to be independent of external beauty if, indeed, they acknowledge this term. I suspect in this "independence," in their total absorption in their own viscera, merely one more performance of a role, one more expression of the self-consciousness that makes the Village more of a show than a reality.

Yet the slow and steady eviction of the artist from Manhattan is, for this tourist, one of the sins of the city most clear in Greenwich Village. If he cannot afford to live there—if the good places with good light are too expensive and the cheap and

makeshift places are threatened by demolition and replacement by luxury flats—where will he go? There is, really, only the Upper West Side, and that, by no stretch of the imagination, can be called a village. Besides, you cannot create overnight what the Village has offered for years. Where else in New York is there a comparable community? Where else can light stream over low houses and books be as plentiful as fruit? Where else can people stroll without direction and meet without planning? If the talk is strange, it is at least not of money. If the faces are strange, they are at least not closed. In the Village people drink wine and coffee rather than martinis, they go to plays more than they look at television, they eat pasta rather than cottage-cheese salads, they walk more than they ride.

And where else in New York is a great green square where in summer guitarists can play and trumpeters blow and old men bend over chess? The grass is dusty, the walks littered, and among the sitters and strollers are deranged and lost and evil faces. But mothers bring their children to play, lovers sit with each other, and those who live within its radius look upon it and say, "This is ours."

Vie
de Bohème

8. *The White Cross*

I BELIEVE in the immortality of rooms. Though it was torn down thirty years ago, I can still walk through the apartment of my youth on Amsterdam Avenue and see every single thing in it. It is suspended in the air, forever held intact through time. One corner of it, seven floors high, looking south on Amsterdam and west to Broadway, is like the bridge of a ship, or a crow's nest. There on a window seat, with the grand piano behind me and the Louvre "Victory" on a pedestal to the left, I looked every evening around six to see my father come out of the subway three blocks away and walk home. All day he taught violin at his settlement school on Third Street, and we—my mother often watched for him with me— would know by his walk what the day had done to him. The thin, tall, graceful figure would either stride those blocks lightly or plod them slowly; his head high or his shoulders stooped. The moment he neared our corner, our white Persian cat (who was not looking) would bound to the front door and wait there till he opened it.

Still there, suspended, is the dining room full of golden oak, the only remembered lapse in taste, where we ate, argued, and studied at night, my brother at calculus while I was subtracting, my brother at Ovid while I was at Thackeray. There, swinging between the folding doors of my passage-bedroom, is the trapeze where I hung. There, at the end of the long dark hall, is the room of my brother, where a sort of pantry exhaled the results of chemical experiment. There, on the other side of this rambling place, is the adult sanctuary of my parents, a small room (inviolable) full of photographs of musicians, affectionately signed. The apartment is full of the sound of music: Brahms and Beethoven and Mozart sonatas halted by arguments in rising voices or played in the serenity of union; Schumann and Rachmaninoff practiced by my brother; my own erratic fumbling at the keys; a quartet, a quintet, a trio with visitors. The air on the seventh floor on Amsterdam Avenue still rings.

Today the city is full of the ghosts of rooms. From some the body has only just departed, the eyes are crossed with white Xs, the dark shell yawns empty behind them. Some have already met with violence and been laid open like skinned animals, their private secrets indecently bare. There by the mounting zigzag of absent stairs, you see the wallpapers, different on every landing. Someone chose the apple blossoms, someone the yellow, someone the green, the pink. "It will go nice with the rug," someone said, or "Let's match the sofa." The open black mouths of fireplaces are there, warming no one.

Some rooms have already gone into the pauper's grave of rubble. But so long as the men and women who live in them are alive, they are as much a part of New York as the glassy cylinders that have supplanted them.

140

What is this daily, hourly loss that the city sustains, and what is the gain it bows to? Last year nearly eleven thousand dwelling units were demolished by wreckers, and the new construction under way or planned involves over seven billion dollars. New York is in the throes of the greatest building boom in its history, a convulsion equal to the wrinkling of the earth's skin by interior forces, a transformation so rapid and so immense that the native of New York becomes a stranger in a new city, all landmarks fled. The little restaurant in the side street, frequented one month ago, is now a hole. The shoemaker's two blocks up is black and empty, awaiting demolition. The walls of a solid-seeming apartment house hide an interior wholly gutted. Where the tailor, the stationer, the florist used to be, where trimmings and pins and ribbons were sold, is a wall made of doors to hide the grinding scoop of the excavator.

What is marked for death in New York? The little, the old, the malfunctioning; the decayed, the unsightly, the verminous; the impractically spacious and the intimately charming; the unexpected, the irregular, the unorthodox. All these are doomed by the inexorable law of economics: the more valuable the land, the more use must be made of it. Against this no other value has power, least of all sentiment and those smaller human pleasures which have sustained man through his immemorial woes.

Exactly what are these pleasures? On Madison Avenue, for instance, five little houses stand on the southeastern end of Sixty-fifth Street. One is blue-

The New York I Know

142

green, one is pink, one is buff, and two are terra-cotta. The moldings, the window spacement, the doorways and the shop fronts are different in each: together they formed a gay and cozy row, inviting the shopper to browse for bags or jewels or china or scarves or antiques, relieving the eye from the upward pressure of height and unbroken façades. The windows of all are crossed with white.

Their doomed counterparts are in nearly every street of the upper East Side, and having once lived in them I know what they have: surprises. White marble Victorian fireplaces with arched and molded openings; very little rooms abutting on very large rooms; strange closets tucked under stairs; back windows opening on patterns of ailanthus and, below, someone else's little garden, sooty but private. In summer these rooms are filled with green light, in winter laced with sun intercepted by branches, or white with a muffling snow. The stairs are steep, the landings not always clean, the plumbing reluctant. The scurrying cockroach rouses a flick of disgust. There is always something to be fixed, something shabby, something broken. There is no valid protection from intruders, no doorman buffer, no one to receive deliveries or bring up the mail. But it is all in human scale, matching the diversities of man, comforting his difference. If there is no protection, there is the compensating freedom from surveillance. Who is to know who turns the key, whose tread is on the stairs, who sleep interlocked, who leaves at dawn? Love feeds on enclosure. What does love do in the brilliant modern lobbies of stone

144

and glass, observed by others? How secret are the hurrying feet down white-lit corridors padded like halls for the insane? The doomed brownstones were better fitted for passion.

They were better fitted for bars. It takes years and the right degree of deterioration to set the mood for a certain kind of drinking. Dark walls, dim lights, scarred mahogany bars, and the long impregnation of smoke and talk and tears and argument and laughter and, above all, of toleration, combined to make the sanctuary of the Third Avenue saloon. Here it is possible both to hide and reveal in company; to nurse impossible grief or unburden unspeakable hurt. Here a man can talk as he never talks to his wife, here a woman can be no better than she knows she is, and often worse. The old bars are forcing grounds for the emotions, escape valves for pressure, areas for personal statement. They house the wisdom of the crazed as well as the aberration of the wise, forming no judgment. They have gone, they are going, they will go. Good riddance, some say: excuses for waste and excess and havens for weakness. Dirty on top of that, and certainly ugly. But where do the harbored go when the harbor's gone? Can they stand the light?

The white cross is on the massively respectable as well; on apartment houses far better built, far kinder to human dimensions than what will supplant them; on the great, sober mansions of the fifty-year-dead rich. Some of them are spared for institutions or diplomacy, but the heavily ornamental masonry of many, so much a part of the old

The New York I Know

New York, so frank a monument to pride in affluence, has already been obliterated except in the minds of the middle-aged men and women who spent their childhoods within them and remember, always, the parties in the ballrooms and the remote seclusion of the nursery. The servants who swept and polished the thirty rooms, who carried trays for endless steps from kitchen to bedroom to dining room to study, are long since dead. They would not mourn the passing of these places, for the kind of pride they felt in their service has died with them, and all they would remember was servitude.

But the white crosses cancel out not only these milder nostalgias along with the many present and positive human values. The wreckers are also deliverers of the city. They scrape out the cancerous tissue of slums, of places long since unfit for human habitation if not for instruments of greed. You can see the Xs now on rows of old dirt-darkened buildings with iron fire escapes scratched across their sullen faces; on the Upper West Side and the Lower East Side, and the Upper East Side, in Harlem, in the West Fifties, in Greenwich Village. Some of these houses sheltered the earlier immigrants, Irish, German, Italian, Czech; but they were newer then and the city was cleaner. There were no parked cars for the garbage and papers to accumulate under, and enough White Wings to accomplish, by the simple efforts of arms and brooms, what mechanized sprinklers and brushers cannot do. And since many of the immigrants came from a tidy and self-respecting middle class, their windows

The White Cross

were washed and their stoops swabbed daily, their hallways painted yearly. But then, they did not live as their inheritors live, four to a room, nor were these rooms left to rot. The newer immigrants have only made worse what was already bad, and the passing of these houses is nothing to mourn. They deface the city and degrade the citizen. And when they are flattened rubble, the great spaces where they used to stand are less like a war-blasted city than like a drawing of deep breath. The openness is a temporary benediction. It is also a reminder of a basic human need which New York cannot afford to satisfy: perspective, the balm of distance. New Yorkers without sight of park or rivers know only foreground; their eyes are forever bullied by the immediate.

It is painful to watch the wrecking of the old and good: when the great iron ball crashes into a fine old cornice it is like a savage blow in a defenseless aging groin. But when it buckles the walls of a filthy tenement with a roaring cascade of bricks and a cloud of dust, the heart leaps up. Smash it, smash it, and clear the ground of evil.

In some ways, the pause between the thunder of ruin and the clatter of rise is the best time of all. The great space cleared for Lincoln Center was filled with promise, where each could imagine the future. The deep holes in Manhattan rock are in themselves fascinating, with water and mud showing in pits and fissures, the excavating jaws gnashing their way through resistant cliffs of stone and rubble, and the helmeted men mysteriously occu-

148

pied on antlike missions. They are timeless; they are building the Pyramids or the Parthenon.

Only they are not. What they do is another kind of miracle: the collective translation of a collective dream, in two dimensions on blue paper, to three dimensions in blue sky. Out of the chaotic depths grows a single organism, a hollow stalagmite that pierces the air.

In the hourly, daily multiplication of this miracle, Manhattan gained in 1959 alone nearly five million square feet of office space and nearly fourteen thousand new housing units, against the eleven demolished; a gain primarily for the rich. Those left homeless by demolition could never afford the luxury units replacing their shelters. Since what was put up is much higher than what was torn down, New York is more steeply vertical than ever before. Yet the tall new buildings alter the profile of the city as a whole much less than they do their immediate context. From the Upper Bay the native New Yorker can spot the new Chase Manhattan shaft, blunting slightly the cluster of pinnacles, and from Central Park the new Equitable Life monolith. But already they seem a natural element of design—so natural that their newness fades the minute they are inhabited and functioning.

It is the *feeling* of New York that they are altering, profoundly, street by street. For the excitement of Manhattan, the optical spur, is diversity, in total contradiction to the prevailing beauty of European capitals, whether London, Paris, or Rome, which is homogeneity. New York has a beat of its

The White Cross

151

own, faster than most but still regular. But as in jazz, the bridging improvisations are in wildly erratic tempi. Even more like the cardiogram of a faulty heart, the eye twitches constantly from low to high to lower to low to higher, leaping one minute from the gabled top of a plaster-fronted four-story house to a forty-eight-story box of steel and glass; from a remodeled brownstone fashionably shorn of cornices to a huge white battlement of luxury flats with jutting terraces. In this planless variety, this incongruity of accident, lies the peculiar fascination of the city—a fascination steadily threatened by the new homogeneity rising about us everywhere.

You have only to look at Park Avenue between Fifty-eighth Street and Forty-seventh Street to know what this is: a shining gantlet of glass, without expression or response. Clean and high and bright and sometimes handsome, like the Lever and Union Carbide Buildings, they are like the surrealist façades of a dream in which oneself, a single figure, runs down infinite vistas crying to be heard. But no one answers. No one can, because these new glass skins are tightly sealed. No window opens, no air flows in, no sound comes out. The people inside are flies in amber: between them and the outer world there is no communication or contact. In all this sterilization and insulation there is, I think, an emotional deadness that not even the bright clean colors and clear sharp forms of the modern interior can circumvent. It is possible that this noncommitment is the perfect atmosphere for the efficient

The New York
I Know

152

functioning of business, of which the new glass buildings rising everywhere are indeed the temples: showcases for the technology of production and selling. For those who work in them, their spanking modernity must be as gratifying as their manifold conveniences. But if their captivity under glass, their insulation in space, does them no harm, I wonder what it does to the outsider who walks by daily. He may be on a stringent visual diet that impoverishes his eye, matched by an emotional malnutrition that contracts his spirit. Whether he knows it or not, he is missing the gentle prods of pleasure that the little old crummy rows, the occasional mansion, the fancy façades once gave him. He has no roughage.

And what of the new apartment houses? I myself live in one of the oldest, with ceilings fourteen feet high, three-foot walls, heavy brass hinges and doorknobs, and, in lobbies and landings, acres of waste space. The kitchen is small but it has a wide-open view, flooded with light. There is only one bathroom, but it is spacious. The elevators rise—slowly —by water power, but with their wood and brass fretwork they look like pavilions rather than coffins. Outside the windows the chubby stone obelisks and ledges and cornices serve no function but the nesting and resting of pigeons, yet without them the distance would lose much enchantment: they are a splendidly incongruous frame for the clean modern slabs far off. Withal, there is a sense of peace and remoteness and refuge in this elaborate old building—almost a removal in time—that bestows dig-

The New York I Know

154

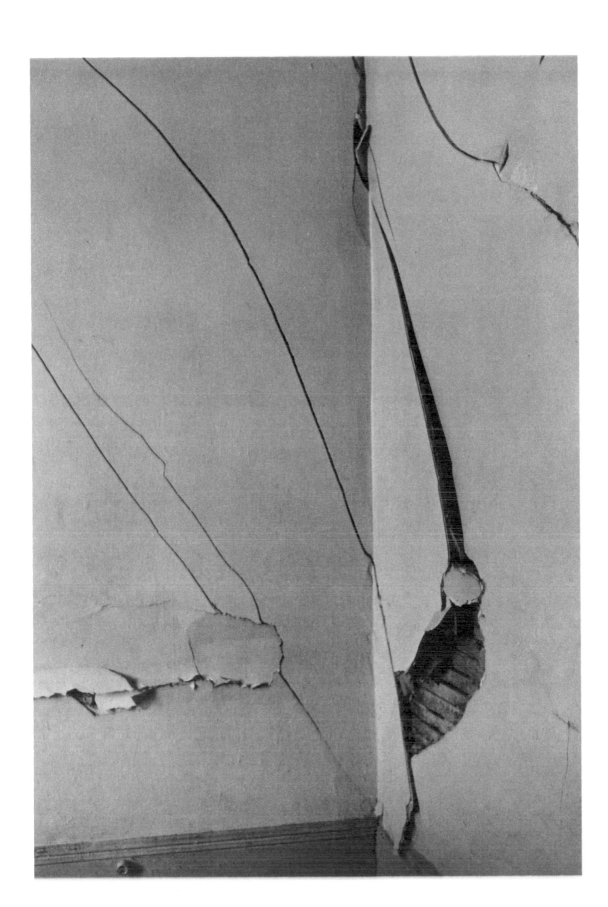

nity on the occupant. He can stand at full stature without touching anything. Or he can sing in full voice and not be heard by his neighbors.

Architects could not—and should not—repeat this pattern now. Economy and aesthetics rule against it and their statements must be new to match the time. But when I visit one of the gleaming white apartment houses recently finished, my appreciation of the new techniques of living, the functional gain, is matched by a sense of poverty. The rooms may be large but they are entirely predictable; there is a distinct limit to what you can do to them, for the dimensions dictate the disposition of furniture. In the old apartment houses, as in brownstones, capricious corners and unexpected hallways allow imagination range: you can do a number of different things in the same space. But the newest apartments strike me like filing cabinets for the human species, one to a drawer, equipped with everything needed for living except that mysterious marriage of man and environment called mood. Space has become mechanical rather than mystical.

The exteriors of these new apartment houses, however, are often vast improvements over their predecessors, particularly the colorless, faceless Park Avenue kind. Manhattan House, on East Sixty-sixth Street, is an exciting block, brilliantly white in the daytime with its jutting terraces, brightly golden at night, with the particular quality of glamour you find in a huge ocean liner with all her lights on in a black sea: the apartments seem to ride the darkened streets. Even in the less imaginative developments, the simple whiteness is good for the New York air and light and sky; it imposes cheer and cleanliness on the neighborhood.

But here too, the gain is matched by a definite loss. The shops on the ground floors of most of these apartment houses are as bright and predictable as their shabby predecessors were cluttered and enticing. Predictably too, their wares are twice as expensive. You cannot browse in this hygienic order, you can only buy: a boon to the seller, no doubt, but a deprivation to the citizen.

It won't be long before all New York is made of these: street after street of modern shops at the foot of great white cliffs, of towering slabs of steel and aluminum and glass that reflect each other and the passing clouds, of walls of dark green glass that look (as they do in the Corning Glass Building) like the solid bank of water that slides with infinite smoothness over the ledge of a dam. All this means excitement and thrust and power and plenty: on a bright November day it is impossible to be unmoved by it, or unconscious of the immense will and effort and talent gone into their building, of the restless vitality filling their interior space.

But it is possible to forget the central core of their meaning to this city: the daily pouring in and out of this narrow throttled island of a million more people who must work, eat, ride, walk, and drive within its confines. Economics makes the builders callous: they think more of profits than people, of the present than the future, of the immediate need than the

The White
Cross

157

ultimate necessity. Only the very few are prepared to pay an enormous price to surround their mammoth towers with open space to let the people breathe: the plazas around the Seagram Building, the court of Lever House, the projected malls and parks of Lincoln Center—these point the way to salvation in what is left to build.

For years, change will be the order of Manhattan, upheaval the climate of all New Yorkers. If this is bracing to promoters and exhilarating to the young, it confuses, tires, and worries the old. The noise, the dirt, and the disruption alone would do this to them, but the shifting of ground under their feet is spiritual as well as physical. They are part of the doomed buildings, and every attack on these is an assault on them. They feel the cataract of crosses on their eyes, and the blind and empty rooms leave their hearts cavernous and deserted. And when the bulldozers finally grind the old houses to dust, their bones are mixed with it.

Perhaps it is just as well. New York is for those without memory: the young.